...rrick

Other titles in the *Shearsman Classics* series:

1. *Poets of Devon and Cornwall, from Barclay to Coleridge*

Forthcoming in the same series:

3. *Spanish Poetry of the Golden Age
        in contemporary English translations* (ed. Tony Frazer)
4. William Strode: *Selected Poems*
5. Sir Thomas Wyatt *Selected Poems*
6. Mary, Lady Chudleigh: *Selected Poems*

Selected Poems

of

Robert Herrick

Selected & edited by
Tony Frazer

Shearsman Books
Exeter

First published in the United Kingdom in 2007 by
Shearsman Books Ltd
58 Velwell Road
Exeter EX4 4LD

www.shearsman.com

ISBN-13 978-1-905700-49-3

ISBN-10 1-905700-49-0

Acknowledgements

The editor wishes to thank Madeleine Corcoran for her assistance with
this project during its initial stages. Any faults that remain are not hers,
but those of the editor.

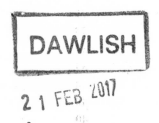

The publisher gratefully acknowledges financial assistance from
Arts Council England.

Contents

Introduction

Robert Herrick (1591-1674) was born the son of a goldsmith in London, and was apprenticed to his uncle, also a goldsmith, at the age of sixteen. After five years of his apprenticeship he went up to Cambridge in 1613 as a fellow commoner, at first studying at Saint John's College, but transferring later to the cheaper Trinity Hall, and graduating in 1617. In the 1620s he joined the group of young poets in London that gathered around the great poet and playwright Ben Jonson, but took holy orders in 1623.

In 1627 he was appointed chaplain to the Duke of Buckingham and took part in his unsuccessful military expedition to La Rochelle. In 1629, a year after his mother's death, Herrick was appointed to the living of Dean Prior, a village on the southern edge of Dartmoor, about half-way between Plymouth and Exeter, which was worth £21 per annum. His first published poem appeared in 1633, but his work would have been circulated in manuscript for many years before this, and not only amongst his immediate circle, or the followers of Jonson.

In view of his royalist sympathies, he was expelled from Dean Prior in 1647, following the overthrow of Charles I, and returned to live in London. He seems to have subsisted there on the charity of his brother Nicholas, as well as friends and supporters such as Mildmay Fane, a fellow-poet and Earl of Westmorland. In 1648, his collected poems *Hesperides* was published in London, and was sold also through a bookseller in Exeter, Thomas Hunt. After the Restoration, Herrick petitioned the King to be reappointed to his post in Dean Prior, and this was granted. From 1660 until his death there in 1674, he served the parish once again as its Vicar.

Such are the bare bones of Herrick's life. It may seem odd that an up-and-coming poet, respected and moving in the best literary circles, should move to such a remote location – London would have been a week's ride away – and stay there for most of the remainder of his life. The reasons are likely to have been economic, rather than devotion to the cloth. He certainly visited London from time to time – a curate in the parish would have permitted his absence – but was no doubt somewhat out of the swim of things in poetic terms, perhaps a little old-fashioned. Rose Macaulay – a direct descendant of Herrick – in her novel about him, *They Were Defeated*, made much of the unfashionable style of his work, and she was almost certainly correct. History, however, has been kinder to Herrick than to some of the then more fashionable writers of his era, and this is despite the fact that it was a golden age for poetry – consider the names of some of his contemporaries: Jonson, Donne, Milton, Herbert, Carew, Vaughan, not to mention fine secondary figures such as Cowley, Waller, Lovelace and Suckling.

Until the late 19th century, Herrick's output – more than 1,400 poems – was under-rated, and some of his more risqué poems were looked at askance by Victorian commentators. However, slowly but surely, his talent as a composer of lyrics has been recognised. But there is more to Herrick than a collection of lyrics, over forty of which were set to music by the composers of his time: his sacred poems, while not plumbing the depths of Donne or Herbert, are still under-rated, and his longer elegiac poems offer a great deal more than one would expect from an acclaimed song-writer and lyric miniaturist. And then his humorous poems and epigrams manage to amuse even now, more than 350 years after their publication. His attitude to Devon was mixed – the poems 'Discontents in Devon' (p.16) and 'His return to London' (p.87) prove that he could be irritated by his provincial isolation – but there are also many poems that also attest to his joy in various aspects of his life in Dean Prior, and to his interest in country life. He was an acute and amusing observer of life in the parish.

The selection here includes a number of the poet's acknow-ledged 'greatest hits', as well as several poems that specifically concern Devon, but it also tries to demonstrate the range of Herrick's work, even while excerpting only a very small percentage of it. The sequence of the poems follows, where possible, that established in the first edition of *Hesperides* in

1648, although, in some cases, shorter poems do appear slightly out of sequence for space reasons. The texts are also based on the 1648 edition, but spelling has been modernised except where this would affect the scansion. The original punctuation – often strange to modern eyes – has been retained, however. The reason for this is that changes can ruin the movement of the verse, and that reading the poems aloud is actually helped by the free-form 17th century punctuation, especially when one compares them with "modernised" editions from the 19th, or early 20th century, which updated the punctuation to then-current norms. The Oxford University Press World's Classics edition (1902, reset 1933, which follows the first edition), has also been consulted in cases where the facsimile of the first edition of *Hesperides* was not sufficiently clear, and the final two poems in the book are also drawn from that edition, as they were not published during Herrick's lifetime. Finally, capitalisation in titles follows that found in the first edition, albeit with modern spelling. Connoisseurs of Herrick's work should note that Oxford University Press has commissioned a two-volume *Complete Poetry of Robert Herrick* for publication in 2010, which is currently being compiled at the University of Newcastle-upon-Tyne. This promises to be the most significant edition of Herrick's poetry in a very long time.

Notes to the poems will be found at the back of the book. This is intended to be a reading edition – hence the decision to update the spelling and to avoid footnotes beneath the poems themselves. A full scholarly apparatus has also been avoided, partly because this would have required a different editor, but also because it would not have been appropriate for a reading edition aimed at a general audience. The notes have been created for the general modern reader, making allowance for the fact that Greek and Roman mythology, and the classical poets, are no longer common currency. My apologies to those who find explanations in the notes for things that they already know far better than I.

Tony Frazer
Exeter, 2007

HESPERIDES:
OR,
THE WORKS
BOTH
HUMANE & DIVINE
OF
ROBERT HERRICK *Esq.*

OVID.

Effugient avidos Carmina noſtra Rogos.

LONDON,
Printed for *John Williams*, and *Francis Egleſfield*,
and are to be ſold by *Tho: Hunt*, Book-ſeller
in *Exon.* 1648.

The Argument of his Book

I sing of brooks, of blossoms, birds, and bowers:
Of April, May, of June, and July-flowers.
I sing of may-poles, hock-carts, wassails, wakes,
Of bridegrooms, brides and of their bridal-cakes.
I write of youth, of love, and have access
By these, to sing of cleanly-wantonness.
I sing of dews, of rains, and piece by piece
Of balm, of oil, of spice and ambergris.
I sing of times trans-shifting; and I write
How roses first came red, and lilies white.
I write of groves, of twilights, and I sing
The court of Mab, and of the fairy king.
I write of Hell; I sing (and ever shall)
Of Heaven, and hope to have it after all.

To his Book

While thou didst keep thy candour undefiled,
Dearly I loved thee; as my first-born child:
But when I saw thee wantonly to roam
From house to house, and never stay at home;
I broke my bonds of love, and bade thee go,
Regardless whether well thou sped'st, or no.
On with thy fortunes then, what e're they be;
If good I'll smile, if bad I'll sigh for thee.

To the Sour Reader

If thou dislik'st the piece thou light'st on first;
Think that of all, that I have writ, the worst:
But if thou read'st my book unto the end,
And still do'st this, and that verse, reprehend:
O perverse man! If all disgustful be,
The extreme scab take thee, and thine, for me.

To his Book

Come thou not near those men, who are like bread
O're-leavened; or like cheese o're-renneted.

The Frozen Heart

I freeze, I freeze, and nothing dwells
In me but snow, and icicles.
For pity's sake give your advice,
To melt this snow, and thaw this ice;
I'll drink down flames, but if so be
Nothing but love can supple me;
I'll rather keep this frost, and snow,
Than to be thawed, or heated so.

To his Mistresses

Help me! help me! now I call
To my pretty witchcrafts all:
Old I am, and cannot do
That, I was accustomed to.
Bring your magics, spells, and charms,
To enflesh my thighs, and arms:
Is there no way to beget
In my limbs their former heat?
Æson had (as poets fain)
Baths that made him young again:
Find that medicine (if you can)
For your dry decrepit man:
Who would fain his strength renew,
Were it but to pleasure you.

To Anthea

If dear Anthea, my hard fate it be
To live some few sad hours after thee:
Thy sacred course with odours I will burn;
And with my laurel crown thy golden urn.
Then holding up (there) such religious things,
As were (time past) thy holy filletings:
Near to thy reverend pitcher I will fall
Down dead for grief, and end my woes withal:
So three in one small plot of ground shall lie,
Anthea, Herrick, and his poetry.

On himself

Young I was, but now am old,
But I am not yet grown cold;
I can play, and I can twine
'Bout a virgin like a vine:
In her lap too I can lie
Melting, and in fancy die:
And return to life, if she
Claps my cheek, or kisseth me;
Thus, and thus it now appears
That our love outlasts our years.

Discontents in Devon

More discontents I never had
    Since I was born, than here;
Where I have been, and still am sad,
    In this dull Devonshire:
Yet justly too I must confess;
    I ne'er invented such
Ennobled numbers for the press,
    Than where I loathed so much.

Cherry-ripe

Cherry-ripe, ripe, ripe, I cry,
Full and fair ones; come and buy:
If so be, you ask me where
They do grow? I answer, there,
Where my Julia's lips do smile;
There's the land, or cherry-isle:
Whose plantations fully show
All the year, where cherries grow.

To Anthea

Now is the time, when all the lights wax dim;
And thou (Anthea) must withdraw from him
Who was thy servant. Dearest, bury me
Under that holy oak, or gospel-tree:
Where (though thou see'st not) thou may'st think upon
Me, when thou yearly go'st procession:
Or for mine honour, lay me in that tomb
In which thy sacred relics shall have room:
For my embalming (sweetest) there will be
No spices wanting, when I'm laid by thee.

Of Love. A Sonnet

How love came in, I do not know,
Whether by th' eye, or ear, or no:
Or whether with the soul it came
(At first) infused with the same:
Whether in part 'tis here or there,
Or, like the soul, whole everywhere:
This troubles me: but I as well
As any other, this can tell;
That when from hence she does depart,
The outlet then is from the heart.

To Anthea

Ah my Anthea! Must my heart still break?
(Love makes me write, what shame forbids to speak.)
Give me a kiss, and to that kiss a score;
Then to that twenty, add a hundred more:
A thousand to that hundred: so kiss on,
To make that thousand up a million.
Treble that million, and when that is done
Let's kiss afresh, as when we first begun.
But yet, though love likes well such scenes as these,
There is an act that will more fully please:
Kissing and glancing, soothing, all make way
But to the acting of this private play:
Name it I would; but being blushing red,
The rest I'll speak, when we meet both in bed.

Dean Bourn, a rude River in Devon by which sometimes he lived

Dean Bourn, farewell; I never look to see
Dean, or thy warty incivility.
Thy rocky bottom, that doth tear thy streams
And makes them frantic, ev'n to all extremes;
To my content, I never should behold,
Were thy streams silver, or thy rocks all gold.
Rocky thou art; and rocky we discover
Thy men; and rocky are thy ways all over.
O men, O manners; now, and ever known
To be a rocky generation!
A people currish; churlish as the seas;
And rude (almost) as rudest salvages,
With whom I did, and may re-sojourn when
Rocks turn to rivers, rivers turn to men.

Duty to Tyrants

Good princes must be prayed for: for the bad
They must be borne with, and in rev'rence had.
Do they first pill thee, next, pluck off thy skin?
Good children kiss the rods, that punish sin.
Touch not the tyrant; let the gods alone
To strike him dead, that but usurps a throne.

A Country life: To his Brother,
Mr. Tho. Herrick

Thrice, and above, blest (my soul's half) art thou,
 In thy both last, and better vow:
Could'st leave the city, for exchange, to see
 The country's sweet simplicity:
And it to know, and practise; with intent
 To grow the sooner innocent:
By studying to know virtue; and to aim
 More at her nature, than her name:
The last is but the least; the first doth tell
 Ways less to live, than to live well:
And both are known to thee, who now canst live
 Led by the conscience; to give
Justice to soon-pleased nature; and to show,
 Wisdom and she together go,
And keep one centre: this with that conspires,
 To teach man to confine desires:
And know, that riches have their proper stint,
 In the contented mind, not mint.
And canst instruct, that those who have the itch
 Of craving more, are never rich.
These things thou know'st to th' height, and dost prevent
 That plague; because thou art content
With that Heav'n gave thee with a wary hand,
 (More blessèd in thy brass, than land)
To keep cheap nature even, and upright;
 To cool, not cocker appetite.
Thus thou canst tearcely live to satisfy
 The belly chiefly; not the eye:
Keeping the barking stomach wisely quiet,
 Less with a neat, than needful diet.
But that which most makes sweet thy country life,
 Is, the fruition of a wife:

Whom (stars consenting with thy fate) thou hast
Got, not so beautiful, as chaste:
By whose warm side thou dost securely sleep
(While love the sentinel doth keep)
With those deeds done by day, which ne'er affright
Thy silken slumbers in the night.
Nor has the darkness power to usher in
Fear to those sheets, that know no sin.
But still thy wife, by chaste intentions led,
Gives thee each night a maidenhead.
The damasked meadows, and the pebbly streams
Sweeten, and make soft your dreams:
The purling springs, groves, birds, and well-weaved bow'rs,
With fields enamelled with flowers,
Present their shapes; while fantasy discloses
Millions of lilies mixed with roses.
Then dream, ye hear the lamb by many a bleat
Wooed to come suck the milky teat:
While Faunus in the vision comes to keep,
From rav'ning wolves, the fleecy sheep.
With thousand such enchanting dreams, that meet
To make sleep not so sound, as sweet:
Nor can these figures so thy rest endear,
As not to rise when Chanticleer
Warns the last watch; but with the dawn dost rise
To work, but first to sacrifice;
Making thy peace with heav'n, for some late fault,
With holy-meal, and spirting-salt.
Which done, thy painful thumb this sentence tells us,
Jove for our labour all things sells us.
Nor are thy daily and devout affairs
Attended with those desp'rate cares,
Th' industrious merchant has; who for to find
Gold, runneth to the Western Inde,
And back again, (tortured with fears) doth fly,

Untaught, to suffer poverty.
But thou at home, blest with securest ease,
　　Sitt'st, and believ'st that there be seas,
And wat'ry dangers; while thy whiter hap,
　　But sees these things within thy map.
And viewing them with a more safe survey
　　Mak'st easy fear unto thee say,
A heart thrice walled with oak, and brass, that man
　　Had, first, durst plough the ocean.
But thou at home without or tide or gale,
　　Canst in thy map securely sail:
Seeing those painted countries; and so guess
　　By those fine shades, their substances:
And from thy compass taking small advice,
　　Buy'st travel at the lowest price.
Nor are thine ears so deaf, but thou canst hear,
　　(Far more with wonder, than with fear)
Fame tell of states, of countries, courts, and kings;
　　And believe there be such things:
When of these truths, thy happier knowledge lies,
　　More in thine ears, than in thine eyes.
And when thou hear'st by that too-true report,
　　Vice rules the most, or all at court:
Thy pious wishes are, (though thou not there)
　　Virtue had, and moved her sphere.
But thou liv'st fearless; and thy face ne'er shows
　　Fortune when she comes, or goes,
But with thy equal thoughts, prepared dost stand,
　　To take her by the either hand;
Nor car'st which comes the first, the foul or fair;
　　A wise man ev'ry way lies square,
And, like a surly oak with storms perplexed;
　　Grows still the stronger, strongly vexed.
Be so, bold spirit; stand centre-like, unmoved;
　　And be not only thought, but proved

To be what I report thee; and inure
    Thyself, if want comes to endure:
And so thou dost: for thy desires are
    Confined to live with private lar:
Not curious whether appetite be fed,
    Or with the first, or second bread.
Who keep'st no proud mouth for delicious cates:
    Hunger makes coarse meats, delicates.
Canst, and unurged, forsake that larded fare,
    Which art, not nature, makes so rare;
To taste boiled nettles, colworts, beets, and eat
    These, and sour herbs, as dainty meat?
While soft opinion makes thy genius say,
    Content makes all ambrosia.
Nor is it that thou keep'st this stricter size
    So much for want, as exercise:
To numb the sense of dearth, which should sin haste it,
    Thou might'st but only see't, not taste it.
Yet can thy humble roof maintain a choir
    Of singing crickets by the fire:
And the brisk mouse may feast herself with crumbs
    Till that the green-eyed kitling comes.
Then to her cabin, blest she can escape
    The sudden danger of a rape.
And thus thy little well-kept stock doth prove,
    Wealth cannot make a life, but love.
Nor art thou so close-handed, but canst spend,
    (Counsel concurring with the end)
As well as spare, still conning o're this theme,
    To shun the first, and last extreme.
Ordaining that thy small stock find no breach,
    Or to exceed thy tether's reach:
But to live round, and close, and wisely true
    To thine own self; and known to few.
Thus let thy rural sanctuary be

Elysium to thy wife and thee;
There to disport yourselves with golden measure:
For seldom use commends the pleasure.
Live, and live blest; thrice happy pair; let breath,
But lost to one, be th' other's death.
And as there is one love, one faith, one troth,
Be so one death, one grave to both.
Till when, in such assurance live, ye may,
Nor fear, or wish your dying day.

The frozen Zone; or, Julia disdainful

Whither? Say, whither shall I fly,
To slake these flames wherein I fry?
To the treasures, shall I go,
Of the rain, frost, hail, and snow?
Shall I search the underground,
Where all damps, and mists are found?
Shall I seek (for speedy ease)
All the floods, and frozen seas?
Or descend into the deep,
Where eternal cold does keep?
These may cool; but there's a zone
Colder yet than any one:
That's my Julia's breast; where dwells
Such destructive icicles;
As that the congelation will
Me sooner starve, than those can kill.

Upon Cuffe. Epig.

Cuffe comes to church much; but he keeps his bed
Those Sundays only, when as briefs are read.
This makes Cuffe dull; and troubles him the most,
Because he cannot sleep i'th' Church, free cost.

Upon Scobble. Epig.

Scobble for whoredom whips his wife; and cries,
He'll slit her nose; but blubb'ring, she replies,
Good sir, make no more cuts i'th' outward skin,
One slit's enough to let adult'ry in.

The Hour-glass

That hour-glass, which there ye see
With water filled, (Sirs, credit me)
The humour was, (as I have read)
But lovers' tears encrystallèd,
Which, as they drop by drop do pass
From th' upper to the under-glass,
Do in a trickling manner tell,
(By many a wat'ry syllable)
That lovers' tears in lifetime shed,
Do restless run when they are dead.

His farewell to Sack

Farewell thou thing, time past so known, so dear
To me, as blood to life and spirit: near,
Nay, thou more near than kindred, friend, man, wife,
Male to the female, soul to body; life
To quick action, or the warm soft side
Of the resigning, yet resisting bride.
The kiss of virgins; first fruits of the bed;
Soft speech, smooth touch, the lips, the maidenhead:
These, and a thousand sweets, could never be
So near, or dear, as thou wast once to me.
O thou the drink of gods, and angels! Wine
That scatter'st spirit and lust; whose purest shine,
More radiant than the summer's sunbeams shows;
Each way illustrious, brave; and like to those
Comets we see by night; whose shagg'd portents
Foretell the coming of some dire events:
Or some full flame, which with a pride aspires,
Throwing about his wild, and active fires.
'Tis thou, above nectar, O divinest soul!
(Eternal in thyself) that can'st control
That, which subverts whole nature, grief and care;
Vexation of the mind, and damned despair.
'Tis thou, alone, who with thy mystic fan,
Work'st more than wisdom, art, or nature can,
To rouse the sacred madness; and awake
The frost-bound blood, and spirits; and to make
Them frantic with thy raptures, flashing through
The soul, like lightning, and as active too.
'Tis not Apollo can, or those thrice three
Castalian sisters, sing, if wanting thee.
Horace, Anacreon, both had lost their fame,
Hads't thou not filled them with thy fire and flame.
Phoebean splendour! and thou Thespian spring!

Of which, sweet swans must drink, before they sing
Their true-paced numbers, and their holy lays,
Which makes them worthy cedar, and the bays.
But why? why longer do I gaze upon
Thee with the eye of admiration?
Since I must leave thee; and enforced, must say
To all thy witching beauties, go, away.
But if thy whimp'ring looks do ask me why?
Then know, that nature bids thee go, not I.
'Tis her erroneous self has made a brain
Uncapable of such a sovereign,
As is thy powerful self. Prithee not smile;
Or smile more inly; lest thy looks beguile
My vows denounced in zeal, which thus much show thee
That I have sworn, but by thy looks to know thee.
Let others drink thee freely; and desire
Thee and their lips espoused; while I admire,
And love thee; but not taste thee. Let my muse
Fail of thy former helps; and only use
Her inadult'rate strength: what's done by me
Hereafter, shall smell of the lamp, not thee.

The suspicion upon his over-much familiarity with a Gentlewoman

And must we part, because some say,
Loud is our love, and loose our play,
And more than well becomes the day?
Alas for pity! and for us
Most innocent, and injured thus!
Had we kept close, or played within,
Suspicion now had been the sin,
And shame had followed long ere this,
T'ave plagued, what now unpunished is.
But we as fearless of the sun,
As faultless; will not wish undone,
What now is done, since *where no sin*
Unbolts the door, no shame comes in.
Then comely and most fragrant maid,
Be you more wary, than afraid
Of these reports; because you see
The fairest most suspected be.
The common forms have no one eye,
Or ear of burning jealousy
To follow them: but chiefly, where
Love makes the cheek, and chin a sphere
To dance and play in: (trust me) there
Suspicion questions every hair.
Come, you are fair; and should be seen
While you are in your sprightful green:
And what though you had been embraced
By me; were you for that unchaste?
No, no, no more than is yond' moon
Which shining in her perfect noon;
In all that great and glorious light,
Continues cold, as is the night.
Then, beauteous maid, you may retire;

And as for me, my chaste desire
Shall move t'wards you; although I see
Your face no more: so live you free
From fame's black lips, as you from me.

Upon the Bishop of Lincoln's Imprisonment

Never was day so over-sick with show'rs,
But that it had some intermitting hours.
Never was night so tedious, but it knew
The last watch out, and saw the dawning too.
Never was dungeon so obscurely deep,
Wherein or light, or day, did never peep.
Never did moon so ebb, or seas so wane,
But they left hope-seed to fill up again.
So you, my Lord, though you have now your stay,
Your night, your prison, and your ebb; you may
Spring up afresh; when all these mists are spent,
And star-like, once more, gild our firmament.
Let but that mighty Caesar speak, and then,
All bolts, all bars, all gates shall cleave; as when
That earthquake shook the house, and gave the stout
Apostles, way (unshackled) to go out.
This, as I wish for, so I hope to see;
Though you (my Lord) have been unkind to me:
To wound my heart, and never to apply,
(When you had power) the meanest remedy:
Well; though my grief by you was galled, the more;
Yet I bring balm and oil to heal your sore.

Dissuasions from Idleness

Cynthius pluck ye by the ear,
That ye may good doctrine hear.
Play not with the maiden-hair;
For each ringlet there's a snare.
Cheek, and eye, and lip, and chin;
These are traps to take fools in.
Arms, and hands, and all parts else,
Are but toils, or manacles
Set on purpose to enthrall
Men, but slothfulls most of all.
Live employed, and so live free
From these fetters; like to me
Who have found, and still can prove,
The lazy man the most doth love.

An Epithalamy to Sir Thomas Southwell and his Lady

I.

Now, now's the time; so oft by truth
Promised should come to crown your youth.
    Then, fair ones, do not wrong
    Your joys, by staying long:
    Or let love's fire go out,
    By ling'ring thus in doubt;
    But learn, that time once lost,
    Is ne'er redeemed by cost.
Then away; come, Hymen guide
To the bed, the bashful bride.

II.

Is it (sweet maid) your fault these holy
Bridal rites go on so slowly?
    Dear, is it this you dread,
    The loss of maidenhead?
    Believe me; you will most
    Esteem it when 'tis lost:
    Then it no longer keep,
    Lest issue lie asleep.
Then away; come, Hymen guide
To the bed, the bashful bride.

III.

These precious pearly purling tears,
But spring from ceremonious fears.
    And 'tis but native shame,
    That hides the loving flame:
    And may a while control

The soft and am'rous soul;
But yet love's fire will wast
Such bashfulness at last.
Then away; come, Hymen guide
To the bed, the bashful bride.

IV.

Night now hath watched herself half blind,
Yet not a maidenhead resigned!
    'Tis strange, ye will not fly
    To love's sweet mystery.
    Might yon full moon the sweets
    Have, promised to your sheets,
    She soon would leave her sphere,
    To be admitted there.
Then away; come, Hymen guide
To the bed, the bashful bride.

V.

On, on devoutly, make no stay;
While Domiduca leads the way:
    And Genius, who attends
    The bed for lucky ends:
    With Juno goes the hours,
    And Graces strewing flowers.
    And the boys with sweet tunes sing,
    Hymen, O Hymen, bring
Home the turtles; Hymen guide
To the bed, the bashful bride.

VI.

Behold! how Hymen's taper-light
Shows you how much is spent of night.

See, see the bridegroom's torch
Half wasted in the porch.
And now those tapers five,
That show the womb shall thrive:
Their silv'ry flames advance,
To tell all prosp'rous chance
Still shall crown the happy life
Of the good man and the wife.

VII.
Move forward then your rosy feet,
And make, whate'er they touch, turn sweet.
May all, like flow'ry meads,
Smell, where your soft foot treads;
And every thing assume
To it, the like perfume:
As Zephyrus when he 'spires
Through woodbine, and sweetbriars.
Then away; come, Hymen guide
To the bed, the bashful bride.

VIII.
And now the yellow veil, at last,
Over her fragrant cheek is cast.
Now seems she to express
A bashful willingness:
Showing a heart consenting;
As with a will repenting.
Then gently lead her on
With wise suspicion:
For that, matrons say, a measure
Of that passion sweetens pleasure.

IX.

You, you that be of her nearest kin,
Now o're the threshold force her in.

    But to avert the worst;
    Let her, her fillets first
    Knit to the posts: this point
    Rememb'ring, to anoint
    The sides: for 'tis a charm
    Strong against future harm:
And the evil deeds, the which
There was hidden by the witch.

X.

O Venus! thou to whom is known
The best way how to loose the zone

    Of virgins! Tell the maid,
    She need not be afraid:
    And bid the youth apply
    Close kisses, if she cry:
    And charge, he not forbears
    Her, though she woo with tears.
Tell them, now they must adventer,
Since that love and night bid enter.

XI.

No fatal owl the bedstead keeps,
With direful notes to fright your sleeps:

    No Furies, here about,
    To put the tapers out,
    Watch, or did make the bed:
    'Tis omen full of dread:
    But all fair signs appear
    Within the chamber here.

Juno here, far off, doth stand,
Cooling sleep with charming wand.

XII.

Virgins, weep not; 'twill come, when,
As she, so you'll be ripe for men.
　　Then grieve her not, with saying
　　She must no more a-maying:
　　Or by rosebuds divine,
　　Who'll be her valentine.
　　Nor name those wanton reaks
　　You've had at barley-breaks.
But now kiss her, and thus say,
Take time Lady while ye may.

XIII.

Now bar the doors, the bridegroom puts
The eager boys to gather nuts.
　　And now, both love and time
　　To their full height do climb:
　　Oh! give them active heat
　　And moisture, both complete:
　　Fit organs for increase,
　　To keep, and to release
That, which may the honoured stem
Circle with a diadem.

XIV.

And now, behold! the bed or couch
That ne'er knew bride's or bridegroom's touch,
　　Feels in itself a fire;
　　And tickled with desire,
　　Pants with a downy breast,

As with a heart possessed:
Shrugging as it did move,
Ev'n with the soul of love.
And (oh!) had it but a tongue,
Doves, 't would say, ye bill too long.

XV.
O enter then! but see ye shun
A sleep, until the act be done.
Let kisses, in their close,
Breathe as the damask rose:
Or sweet, as is that gum
Doth from Panchaia come.
Teach nature now to know,
Lips can make cherries grow
Sooner, than she, ever yet,
In her wisdom could beget.

XVI.
On your minutes, hours, days, months, years,
Drop the fat blessing of the spheres.
That good, which Heav'n can give
To make you bravely live;
Fall, like a spangling dew,
By day, and night on you.
May fortune's lily-hand
Open at your command;
With all lucky birds to side
With the bridegroom, and the bride.

XVII.
Let bounteous Fate your spindles full
Fill, and wind up with whitest wool.

Let them not cut the thread
Of life, until ye bid.

May death yet come at last;
And not with desp'rate hast:
But when ye both can say,
Come, let us now away.
Be ye to the barn then borne,
Two, like two ripe shocks of corn.

To a Gentlewoman
objecting to him his grey hairs

Am I despised, because you say,
And I dare swear, that I am grey?
Know, Lady, you have but your day:
And time will come when you shall wear
Such frost and snow upon your hair:
And when (though long it comes to pass)
You question with your looking-glass;
And in that sincere crystal seek,
But find no rose-bud in your cheek:
Nor any bed to give the shew
Where such a rare carnation grew.
Ah! then too late, close in your chamber keeping,
    It will be told
    That you are old;
By those true tears y'are weeping.

The cruel Maid

And cruel maid, because I see
You scornful of my love, and me:
I'll trouble you no more; but go
My way, where you shall never know.
What is become of me: there I
Will find me out a path to die;
Or learn some way how to forget
You, and your name, for ever: yet,
Ere I go hence; know this from me,
What will, in time, your fortune be:
This to your coyness I will tell;
And having spoke it once, farewell.
The lily will not long endure;
Nor the snow continue pure:
The rose, the violet, one day
See, both these lady-flowers decay:
And you must fade, as well as they.
And it may chance that love may turn,
And (like to mine) make your heart burn
And weep to see't; yet this thing do,
That my last vow commends to you:
When you shall see that I am dead,
For pity let a tear be shed;
And (with your mantle o're me cast)
Give my cold lips a kiss at last:
If twice you kiss, you need not fear,
That I shall stir, or live more here.
Next, hollow out a tomb to cover
Me; me, the most despisèd lover:
And write thereon, *This, reader, know:*
Love killed this man. No more, but so.

His misery in a Mistress

Water, water I espy:
Come, and cool ye; all who fry
In your loves; but none as I.

Though a thousand show'rs be
Still a-falling, yet I see
Not one drop to light on me.

Happy you, who can have seas
For to quench ye, or some ease
From your kinder mistresses.

I have one, and she alone,
Of a thousand thousand known,
Dead to all compassion.

Such an one, as will repeat
Both the cause, and make the heat
More by provocation great.

Gentle friends, though I despair
Of my cure, do you beware
Of those girls, which cruel are.

Distrust

To safeguard man from wrongs, there nothing must
Be truer to him, then a wise distrust.
And to thyself be best this sentence known,
Hear all men speak; but credit few or none.

To Jos: Lord Bishop of Exeter

Whom should I fear to write to, if I can
Stand before you, my learned diocesan?
And never show blood-guiltiness, or fear
To see my lines excathedrated here.
Since none so good are, but you may condemn;
Or here so bad, but you may pardon them.
If then, (my Lord) to sanctify my muse
One only poem out of all you'll choose;
And mark it for a rapture nobly writ,
'Tis good confirmed; for you have bishoped it.

To the Detractor

Where others love, and praise my verses; still
Thy long black thumbnail marks 'em out for ill:
A fellon take it, or some whitflaw come
For to unslate, or to untile that thumb!
But cry thee mercy: exercise thy nails
To scratch or claw, so that thy tongue not rails:
Some numbers prurient are, and some of these
Are wanton with their itch; scratch, and 'twill please.

To his Book

Like to a bride, come forth my book, at last,
With all thy richest jewels overcast:
Say, if there be 'mongst many gems here; one
Deserveless of the name of paragon;
Blush not at all for that; since we have set
Some pearls on queens, that have been counterfeit.

Corinna's going a-Maying

Get up, get up for shame, the blooming morn
Upon her wings presents the god unshorn.
    See how Aurora throws her fair
    Fresh-quilted colours through the air:
    Get up, sweet slug-a-bed, and see
    The dew-bespangling herb and tree.
Each flower has wept, and bowed toward the east,
Above an hour since; yet you not dressed,
    Nay! not so much as out of bed?
    When all the birds have matins said,
    And sung their thankful hymns: 'tis sin,
    Nay, profanation to keep in,
When as a thousand virgins on this day,
Spring, sooner than the lark, to fetch in May.

Rise; and put on your foliage, and be seen
To come forth, like the spring-time, fresh and green;
    And sweet as Flora. Take no care
    For jewels for your gown, or hair:
    Fear not; the leaves will strew
    Gems in abundance upon you:
Besides, the childhood of the day has kept,
Against you come, some orient pearls unwept:
    Come, and receive them while the light
    Hangs on the dew-locks of the night:
    And Titan on the eastern hill
    Retires himself, or else stands still
Till you come forth. Wash, dress, be brief in praying:
Few beads are best, when once we go a-maying.

Come, my Corinna, come; and coming, mark
How each field turns a street; each street a park
    Made green, and trimmed with trees: see how

Devotion gives each house a bough,
Or branch: each porch, each door, ere this,
An ark a tabernacle is
Made up of whitethorn neatly interwove;
As if here were those cooler shades of love.
Can such delights be in the street,
And open fields, and we not see't?
Come, we'll abroad; and let's obey
The proclamation made for May:
And sin no more, as we have done, by staying:
But my Corinna, come, let's go a-maying.

There's not a budding boy, or girl, this day,
But is got up, and gone to bring in May.
A deal of youth, ere this, is come
Back, and with whitethorn laden home.
Some have despatched their cakes and cream,
Before that we have left to dream:
And some have wept, and wooed, and plighted troth,
And chose their priest, ere we can cast off sloth:
Many a green-gown has been given;
Many a kiss, both odd and even:
Many a glance too has been sent
From out the eye, love's firmament:
Many a jest told of the keys betraying
This night, and locks picked, yet we're not a-maying.

Come, let us go, while we are in our prime;
And take the harmless folly of the time.
We shall grow old apace, and die
Before we know our liberty.
Our life is short; and our days run
As fast away as does the sun;
And as a vapour, or a drop of rain
Once lost, can ne'r be found again:

So when or you or I are made
A fable, song, or fleeting shade;
All love, all liking, all delight
Lies drowned with us in endless night.
Then while time serves, and we are but decaying;
Come, my Corinna, come, let's go a-maying.

To his dying Brother, Master William Herrick

Life of my life, take not so soon thy flight,
But stay the time till we have bade good-night.
Thou hast both wind and tide with thee; thy way
As soon dispatched is by the night, as day.
Let us not then so rudely henceforth go
Till we have wept, kissed, sighed, shook hands, or so.
There's pain in parting; and a kind of hell,
When once true lovers take their last farewell.
What? shall we two our endless leaves take here
Without a sad look, or a solemn tear?
He knows not love, that hath not this truth proved,
Love is most loth to leave the thing beloved.
Pay we our vows, and go; yet when we part,
Then, even then, I will bequeath my heart
Into thy loving hands: for I'll keep none
To warm my breast, when thou my pulse art gone.
No, here I'll last, and walk (a harmless shade),
About this urn, wherein thy dust is laid,
To guard it so, as nothing here shall be
Heavy, to hurt those sacred seeds of thee.

The Welcome to Sack

So soft streams meet, so springs with gladder smiles
Meet after long divorcement by the isles:
When love (the child of likeness) urgeth on
Their crystal natures to an union.
So meet stol'n kisses, when the moony nights
Call forth fierce lovers to their wished delights:
So Kings & Queens meet, when desire convinces
All thoughts, but such as aim at getting princes,
As I meet thee. Soul of my life, and fame!
Eternal lamp of love! whose radiant flame
Out-glares the heav'ns' Osiris; and thy gleams
Outshine the splendour of his mid-day beams.
Welcome, O welcome my illustrious spouse;
Welcome as are the ends unto my vows:
I! far more welcome then the happy soil,
The sea-scourged merchant, after all his toil,
Salutes with tears of joy; when fires betray
The smoky chimneys of his Ithaca.
Where hast thou been so long from my embraces,
Poor pitied exile? Tell me, did thy graces
Fly discontented hence, and for a time
Did rather choose to bless another clime?
Or went'st thou to this end, the more to move me,
By thy short absence, to desire and love thee?
Why frowns my sweet? Why won't my Saint confer
Favours on me, her fierce idolater?
Why are those looks, those looks the which have been
Time-past so fragrant, sickly now drawn in
Like a dull twilight? Tell me; and the fault
I'll expiate with sulphur, hair, and salt:
And with the crystal humour of the spring,
Purge hence the guilt, and kill this quarrelling.
Would thou not smile, or tell me what's amiss?

Have I been cold to hug thee, too remiss,
Too temp'rate in embracing? Tell me, has desire
To thee-ward died i'th'embers, and no fire
Left in this raked-up ash-heap, as a mark
To testify the glowing of a spark?
Have I divorced thee only to combine
In hot adult'ry with another wine?
True, I confess I left thee, and appeal
'Twas done by me, more to confirm my zeal,
And double my affection on thee; as do those,
Whose love grows more enflamed, by being foes.
But to forsake thee ever, could there be
A thought of such like possibility?
When thou thyself dare'st say, thy isles shall lack
Grapes, before Herrick leaves Canary sack.
Thou mak'st me airy, active to be born,
Like Iphyclus, upon the tops of corn.
Thou mak'st me nimble, as the wingèd hours,
To dance and caper on the heads of flowers,
And ride the sunbeams. Can there be a thing
Under the heavenly Isis, that can bring
More love unto my life, or can present
My genius with a fuller blandishment?
Illustrious idol! could th'Egyptians seek
Help from the garlic, onion, and the leek,
And pay no vows to thee? who wast their best
God, and far more transcendent then the rest?
Had Cassius, that weak water-drinker, known
Thee in thy vine, or had but tasted one
Small chalice of thy frantic liquor; he
As the wise Cato had approved of thee.
Had not Jove's son, that brave Tyrinthian swain,
(Invited to the Thespian banquet) ta'ne
Full goblets of thy gen'rous blood; his spright
Ne'r had kept heat for fifty maids that night.

Come, come and kiss me; love and lust commends
Thee, and thy beauties; kiss, we will be friends,
Too strong for fate to break us: look upon
Me, with that full pride of complexion,
As Queens, meet Queens; or come thou unto me,
As Cleopatra came to Antony;
When her high carriage did at once present
To the Triumvir, love and wonderment.
Swell up my nerves with spirit; let my blood
Run through my veins, like to a hasty flood.
Fill each part full of fire, active to do
What thy commanding soul shall put it to.
And till I turn apostate to thy love,
Which here I vow to serve, do not remove
Thy fires from me; but Apollo's curse
Blast these-like actions, or a thing that's worse;
When these circumstants shall but live to see
The time that I prevaricate from thee.
Call me *the son of beer*, and then confine
Me to the tap, the toast, the turf; let wine
Ne'r shine upon me; may my numbers all
Run to a sudden death, and funeral.
And last, when thee (dear spouse) I disavow,
Ne'r may prophetic Daphne crown my brow.

Impossibilities to his friend

My faithful friend, if you can see
The fruit to grow up, or the tree:
If you can see the colour come
Into the blushing pear, or plum:
If you can see the water grow
To cakes of ice, or flakes of snow:
If you can see, that drop of rain
Lost in the wild sea, once again:
If you can see, how dreams do creep
Into the brain by easy sleep:
Then there is hope that you may see
Her love me once, who now hates me.

Upon Luggs. Epig.

Luggs, by the condemnation of the bench,
Was lately whipped for lying with a wench.
Thus pains and pleasures turn by turn succeed:
He smarts at last, who does not first take heed.

Upon Bunce. Epig.

Money thou ow'st me; prithee fix a day
For payment promised, though thou never pay:
Let it be Doomsday; nay, take longer scope;
Pay when th'art honest; let me have some hope.

To live merrily, and to trust to Good Verses

Now is the time for mirth,
   Nor cheek, or tongue be dumb:
For with the flow'ry earth,
   The golden pomp is come.

The golden pomp is come;
   For now each tree does wear
(Made of her pap and gum)
   Rich beads of amber here.

Now reigns the rose, and now
   Th' Arabian dew besmears
My uncontrollèd brow,
   And my retorted hairs.

Homer, this health to thee,
   In sack of such a kind,
That it would make thee see,
   Though thou wert ne'r so blind.

Next, Virgil, I'll call forth,
   To pledge this second health
In wine, whose each cup's worth
   An Indian commonwealth.

A goblet next I'll drink
   To Ovid; and suppose,
Made he the pledge, he'd think
   The world had all one nose.

Then this immensive cup
   Of aromatic wine,

Catullus, I quaff up
   To that terse muse of thine.

Wild I am now with heat;
   O Bacchus! cool thy rays!
Or frantic I shall eat
   Thy thyrse, and bite the bays.

Round, round, the roof does run;
   And being ravished thus,
Come, I will drink a tun
   To my Propertius.

Now, to Tibullus, next,
   This flood I drink to thee:
But stay; I see a text,
   That this presents to me.

Behold, Tibullus lies
   Here burnt, whose small return
Of ashes, scarce suffice
   To fill a little urn.

Trust to good verses then;
   They only will aspire,
When pyramids, as men,
   Are lost, i'th'funeral fire.

And when all bodies meet
   In Lethe to be drowned;
Then only numbers sweet,
   With endless life are crowned.

To the Virgins, to make much of Time

Gather ye rosebuds while ye may,
    Old time is still a-flying:
And this same flower that smiles today,
    Tomorrow will be dying.

The glorious lamp of heaven, the sun,
    The higher he's a-getting;
The sooner will his race be run,
    And nearer he's to setting.

That age is best, which is the first,
    When youth and blood are warmer;
But being spent, the worse, and worst
    Times, still succeed the former.

Then be not coy, but use your time;
    And while ye may, go marry:
For having lost but once your prime,
    You may for ever tarry.

A Meditation for his Mistress

You are a tulip seen today,
But (dearest) of so short a stay;
That where you grew, scarce man can say.

You are a lovely July-flower,
Yet one rude wind, or ruffling shower,
Will force you hence, (and in an hour.)

You are a sparkling rose i'th' bud,
Yet lost, ere that chaste flesh and blood
Can show where you or grew, or stood.

You are a full-spread fair-set vine,
And can with tendrils love entwine,
Yet dried, ere you distill your wine.

You are like balm enclosed (well)
In amber, or some crystal shell,
Yet lost ere you transfuse your smell.

You are a dainty violet,
Yet withered, ere you can be set
Within the virgin's coronet.

You are the queen all flowers among,
But die you must (fair maid) ere long,
As he, the maker of this song.

The bleeding hand:
or, The sprig of Eglantine given to a maid

From this bleeding hand of mine,
Take this sprig of eglantine.
Which (though sweet unto your smell)
Yet the fretful briar will tell,
He who plucks the sweets shall prove
Many thorns to be in love.

Upon Julia's breasts

Display thy breasts, my Julia, there let me
Behold that circummortal purity:
Between whose glories, there my lips I'll lay,
Ravished, in that fair *Via Lactea*.

No Lock against Lechery

Bar close as you can, and bolt fast too your door,
To keep out the lecher, and keep in the whore:
Yet, quickly you'll see by the turn of a pin,
The whore to come out, or the lecher come in.

To the Rose. Song.

Go, happy rose, and interwove
With other flowers, bind my love.
    Tell her, too, she must not be,
    Longer flowing, longer free,
    That so oft has fettered me.

Say (if she's fretful) I have bands
Of pearl, and gold, to bind her hands:
    Tell her, if she struggle still,
    I have myrtle rods, (at will)
    For to tame, though not to kill.

Take thou my blessing, thus, and go,
And tell her this, but do not so,
    Lest a handsome anger fly,
    Like a lightning, from her eye,
    And burn thee up, as well as I.

The Hock-cart, or Harvest home: To The Right Honourable, Mildmay, Earl of Westmorland

Come sons of summer, by whose toil,
We are the lords of wine and oil:
By whose tough labours, and rough hands,
We rip up first, then reap our lands.
Crowned with the ears of corn, now come,
And, to the pipe, sing harvest home.
Come forth, my lord, and see the cart
Dressed up with all the country art.
See, here a maukin, there a sheet,
As spotless pure, as it is sweet:
The horses, mares, and frisking fillies,
(Clad, all, in linen, white as lilies.)
The harvest swains, and wenches bound
For joy, to see the hock-cart crowned.
About the cart, hear, how the rout
Of rural younglings raise the shout;
Pressing before, some coming after,
Those with a shout, and these with laughter.
Some bless the cart; some kiss the sheaves;
Some prank them up with oaken leaves:
Some cross the fill-horse; some with great
Devotion, stroke the home-borne wheat:
While other rustics, less attent
To prayers, than to merriment,
Run after with their breeches rent.
Well, on, brave boys, to your lord's hearth,
Glitt'ring with fire; where, for your mirth,
Ye shall see first the large and chief
Foundation of your feast, fat beef:
With upper storeys, mutton, veal
And bacon, which makes full the meal,

With sev'ral dishes standing by,
As here a custard, there a pie,
And here, all tempting frumenty.
And for to make the merry cheer,
If smirking wine be wanting here,
There's that, which drowns all care, stout beer:
Which freely drink to your Lord's health
Then to the plough, (the commonwealth)
Next to your flails, your fanes, your fats;
Then to the maids with wheaten hats:
To the rough sickle, and crook'd scythe,
Drink frolic boys, till all be blithe.
Feed, and grow fat; and as ye eat,
Be mindful, that the lab'ring neat,
(As you) may have their fill of meat.
And know, besides, ye must revoke
The patient ox unto the yoke,
And all go back unto the plough
And harrow, (though they're hanged up now.)
And, you must know, your Lord's word's true,
Feed him ye must, whose food fills you.
And that this pleasure is like rain,
Not sent ye for to drown your pain,
But for to make it spring again.

Upon the death of his Sparrow. An Elegy

Why do not all fresh maids appear
To work love's sampler only here,
Where springtime smiles throughout the year?
Are not here rosebuds, pinks, all flowers,
Nature begets by th' sun and showers,
Met in one hearse-cloth, to o'respread
The body of the under-dead?
Phil, the late dead, the late dead dear,
O! may no eye distil a tear
For you once lost, who weep not here!
Had Lesbia (too-too-kind) but known
This sparrow, she had scorned her own:
And for this dead which under lies
Wept out her heart, as well as eyes.
But endless peace, sit here, and keep
My Phil, the time he has to sleep,
And thousand virgins come and weep,
To make these flow'ry carpets show
Fresh, as their blood; and ever grow,
Till passengers shall spend their doom,
Not Virgil's gnat had such a tomb.

How Roses came red

Roses at first were white,
    Till they could not agree,
Whether my Sappho's breast,
    Or they more white should be.

But being vanquished quite,
    A blush their cheeks bespread;
Since which (believe the rest)
    The roses first came red.

To the Willow-tree

Thou art to all lost love the best,
    The only true plant found,
Wherewith young men and maids distressed,
    And left of love, are crowned.

When once the lovers' rose is dead,
    Or laid aside forlorn;
Then willow-garlands, 'bout the head,
    Bedewed with tears, are worn.

When with neglect, (the lovers' bane)
    Poor maids rewarded be,
For their love lost; their only gain
    Is but a wreath from thee.

And underneath thy cooling shade,
    (When weary of the light)
The love-spent youth, and love-sick maid,
    Come to weep out the night.

To Anthea, who may command him anything

Bid me to live, and I will live
    Thy Protestant to be:
Or bid me love, and I will give
    A loving heart to thee.

A heart as soft, a heart as kind,
    A heart as sound and free,
As in the whole world thou canst find,
    That heart I'll give to thee.

Bid that heart stay, and it will stay,
    To honour thy decree:
Or bid it languish quite away,
    And't shall do so for thee.

Bid me to weep, and I will weep,
    While I have eyes to see:
And having none, yet I will keep
    A heart to weep for thee.

Bid me despair, and I'll despair,
    Under that cypress tree:
Or bid me die, and I will dare
    E'en death, to die for thee.

Thou art my life, my love, my heart,
    The very eyes of me:
And hast command of every part,
    To live and die for thee.

To Meadows

Ye have been fresh and green,
    Ye have been filled with flowers:
And ye the walks have been
    Where maids have spent their hours.

You have beheld, how they
    With wicker arks did come
To kiss, and bear away
    The richer cowslips home.

Y'ave heard them sweetly sing,
    And seen them in a round:
Each virgin, like a spring,
    With honeysuckles crowned.

But now, we see, none here,
    Whose silv'ry feet did tread,
And with dishevelled hair,
    Adorned this smoother mead.

Like unthrifts, having spent,
    Your stock, and needy grown,
Y'are left here to lament
    Your poor estates, alone.

No fault in women

No fault in women to refuse
The offer, which they most would choose.
No fault in women, to confess
How tedious they are in their dress.
No fault in women, to lay on
The tincture of vermilion:
And there to give the cheek a dye
Of white, where nature doth deny.
No fault in women, to make show
Of largeness, when th'are nothing so:
(When true it is the outside swells
With inward buckram, little else.)
No fault in women, though they be
But seldom from suspicion free:
No fault in womankind, at all,
If they but slip and never fall.

To Virgins

Hear ye virgins, and I'll teach,
What the times of old did preach.
Rosamond was in a bower
Kept, as Danae in a tower:
But yet love (who subtle is)
Crept to that, and came to this.
Be ye locked up like to these,
Or the rich Hesperides;
Or those babies in your eyes,
In their crystal nunneries;
Notwithstanding love will win,
Or else force a passage in:
And as coy be, as you can,
Gifts will get ye, or the man.

The Entertainment: or, Porch-verse, at the Marriage of Mr. Hen. Northly, and the most witty Mrs. Lettice Yard

Welcome! but yet no entrance, till we bless
First you, then you, and both for white success.
Profane no porch young man and maid, for fear
Ye wrong the threshold-god, that keeps peace here:
Please him, and then all good luck will betide
You, the brisk bridegroom, you the dainty bride.
Do all things sweetly, and in comely wise;
Put on your garlands first, then sacrifice:
That done; when both of you have seemly fed,
We'll call on night, to bring ye both to bed:
Where, being laid, all fair signs looking on,
Fish-like, increase then to a million:
And millions of springtimes may ye have,
Which spent, one death, bring to ye both one grave.

Her Legs

Fain would I kiss my Julia's dainty leg,
Which is as white and hairless as an egg.

To the most fair and lovely Mistress, Anne Soame, now Lady Abdie

So smell those odours that do rise
From out the wealthy spiceries;
So smells the flow'r of blooming clove,
Or roses smothered in the stove;
So smells the air of spicèd wine;
Or essences of jessamine:
So smells the breath about the hives,
When well the work of honey thrives;
And all the busy factors come
Laden with wax and honey home:
So smell those neat and woven bowers,
All over-arched with orange flowers,
And almond blossoms, that do mix
To make rich these aromatics:
So smell those bracelets, and those bands
Of amber chafed between the hands,
When thus enkindled they transpire
A noble perfume from the fire.
The wine of cherries, and to these,
The cooling breath of respasses;
The smell of morning's milk and cream;
Butter of cowslips mixed with them;
Of roasted warden, or baked pear,
These are not to be reckoned here,
When as the meanest part of her,
Smells like the maiden pomander.
Thus sweet she smells, or what can be
More liked by her, or loved by me.

Upon M. Ben Jonson. Epig.

After the rare arch-poet Jonson died,
The sock grew loathsome, and the buskin's pride,
Together with the stage's glory stood
Each like a poor and pitied widowhood.
The cirque profaned was; and all postures racked:
For men did strut, and stride, and stare, not act.
Then temper flew from words; and men did squeak,
Look red, and blow, and bluster, but not speak:
No holy rage, or frantic fires did stir,
Or flash about the spacious theatre.
No clap of hands, or shout, or praise's proof
Did crack the playhouse sides, or cleave her roof.
Artless the scene was; and that monstrous sin
Of deep and arrant ignorance came in;
Such ignorance as theirs was, who once hissed
At thy unequalled play, the *Alchemist*:
Oh fie upon 'em! Lastly too, all wit
In utter darkness did, and still will sit
Sleeping the luckless age out, till that she
Her resurrection has again with thee.

To his Book

Have I not blessed thee? Then go forth; nor fear
Or spice, or fish, or fire, or close-stools here.
But with thy fair fates leading thee, go on
With thy most white predestination.
Nor think these ages that do hoarsely sing
The farting tanner, and familiar king;
The dancing friar, tattered in the bush;
Those monstrous lies of little Robin Rush:
Tom Chipperfield, and pretty lisping Ned,
That doted on a maid of gingerbread:
The flying pilchard, and the frisking dace,
With all the rabble of Tim Trundell's race,
(Bred from the dunghills, and adulterous rhymes,)
Shall live, and thou not superlast all times?
No, no, thy stars have destined thee to see
The whole world die, and turn to dust with thee.
He's greedy of his life, who will not fall,
When as a public ruin bears down all.

Upon Parson Beanes

Old Parson Beanes hunts six days of the week,
And on the seventh, he has his notes to seek.
Six days he hollows so much breath away
That on the seventh, he can nor preach, or pray.

The mad Maid's Song

Good morrow to the day so fair;
    Good morning sir to you:
Good morrow to mine own torn hair,
    Bedabbled with the dew.

Good morning to this primrose too;
    Good morrow to each maid;
That will with flowers the tomb bestrew,
    Wherein my love is laid.

Ah woe is me, woe, woe is me,
    Alack and well-a-day!
For pity, sir, find out that bee,
    Which bore my love away.

I'll seek him in your bonnet brave;
    I'll seek him in your eyes;
Nay, now I think th'ave made his grave
    I'th'bed of strawberries.

I'll seek him there; I know, ere this,
    The cold, cold earth doth shake him;
But I will go, or send a kiss
    By you, sir, to awake him.

Pray hurt him not; though he be dead,
    He knows well who do love him,
And who with green turfs rear his head,
    And who do rudely move him.

He's soft and tender (pray take heed)
    With bands of cowslips bind him;
And bring him home, but 'tis decreed,
    That I shall never find him.

Upon the Nipples of Julia's Breast

Have ye beheld (with much delight)
A red rose peeping through a white?
Or else a cherry (double graced)
Within a lily? Centre placed?
Or ever marked the pretty beam,
A strawberry shows half-drowned in cream?
Or seen rich rubies blushing through
A pure smooth pearl, and orient too?
So like to this, nay all the rest,
Is each neat niplet of her breast.

To the little Spinners

Ye pretty housewives, would ye know
The work that I would put ye to?
This, this it should be, for to spin,
A lawn for me, so fine and thin,
As it might serve me for my skin.
For cruel love has me so whipped,
That of my skin, I all am stripped;
And shall despair, that any art
Can ease the rawness, or the smart;
Unless you skin again each part.
Which mercy if you will but do,
I call all maids to witness too
What here I promise, that no broom
Shall now, or ever after come
To wrong a spinner or her loom.

To Groves

Ye silent shades, whose each tree here
Some relic of a saint doth wear:
Who for some sweetheart's sake, did prove
The fire, and martyrdom of love.
Here is the legend of those saints
That died for love; and their complaints:
Their wounded hearts; and names we find
Encarved upon the leaves and rind.
Give way, give way to me, who come
Scorched with the selfsame martyrdom:
And have deserved as much (love knows)
As to be canonised 'mongst those,
Whose deeds, and deaths here written are
Within your greeny calendar:
By all those virgins' fillets hung
Upon your boughs, and requiems sung
For saints and souls departed hence,
(Here honoured still with frankincense)
By all those tears that have been shed,
As a drink-offering, to the dead:
By all those true-love knots, that be
With mottoes carved on every tree,
By sweet Saint Phyllis; pity me:
By dear Saint Iphis; and the rest
Of all those other saints now blessed;
Me, me, forsaken, here admit
Among your myrtles to be writ:
That my poor name may have the glory
To live remembered in your story.

To the right Honourable Mildmay,
Earl of Westmorland

You are a lord, an earl, nay more, a man,
Who writes sweet numbers well as any can:
If so, why then are not these verses hurled,
Like sibyl's leaves, throughout the ample world?
What is a jewel if it be not set
Forth by a ring, or some rich carcanet?
But being so; then the beholders cry,
See, see a gem as rare as Belus' eye.
Then public praise does run upon the stone,
For a most rich, a rare, a precious one.
Expose your jewels then unto the view,
That we may praise them, or themselves prize you.
Virtue concealed (with Horace you'll confess)
Differs not much from drowsy slothfulness.

The parting Verse, or charge to his supposed Wife when he travelled

Go hence, and with this parting kiss,
Which joins two souls, remember this;
Though thou beest young, kind, soft, and fair,
And mayst draw thousands with a hair:
Yet let these glib temptations be
Furies to others, friends to me.
Look upon all; and though on fire
Thou setst their hearts, let chaste desire
Steer thee to me; and think (me gone)
In having all, that thou hast none.
Nor so immured would I have
Thee live, as dead and in thy grave;
But walk abroad, yet wisely well
Stand for my coming, sentinel.
And think (as thou dost walk the street)
Me, or my shadow thou dost meet.
I know a thousand greedy eyes
Will on thy feature tyrannise,
In my short absence; yet behold
Them like some picture, or some mould
Fashioned like thee; which, though 't'ave ears
And eyes, it neither sees or hears.
Gifts will be sent, and letters, which
Are the expressions of that itch
And salt, which frets thy suitors; fly
Both, lest thou lose thy liberty:
For that once lost, thou't fall to one,
Than prostrate to a million.
But if they woo thee, do thou say,
(As that chaste Queen of Ithaca
Did to her suitors) this web done
(Undone as oft as done) I'm won;

I will not urge thee, for I know,
Though thou art young, thou canst say no,
And no again, and so deny,
Those thy lust-burning incubi.
Let them enstyle thee fairest fair,
The pearl of princes, yet despair
That so thou art, because thou must
Believe, love speaks it not, but lust;
And this their flatt'ry does commend
Thee chiefly for their pleasure's end.
I am not jealous of thy faith,
Or will be; for the axiom saith,
He that doth suspect, does haste
A gentle mind to be unchaste.
No, live thee to thy self, and keep
Thy thoughts as cold, as is thy sleep:
And let thy dreams be only fed
With this, that I am in thy bed.
And thou then turning in that sphere,
Waking shalt find me sleeping there.
But yet if boundless lust must scale
Thy fortress, and will needs prevail;
And wildly force a passage in,
Banish consent, and 'tis no sin
Of thine; so Lucrece fell, and the
Chaste Syracusian Cyane.
So Medullina fell, yet none
Of these had imputation
For the least trespass; 'cause the mind
Here was not with the act combined.
The body sins not, 'tis the will
That makes the action, good, or ill.
And if thy fall should this way come,
Triumph in such a martyrdom.
I will not over-long enlarge

To thee, this my religious charge.
Take this compression, so by this
Means, I shall know what other kiss
Is mixed with mine; and truly know,
Returning, if 't be mine or no:
Keep it till then; and now my spouse,
For my wished safety pay thy vows,
And prayers to Venus; if it please
The great blue ruler of the seas;
Not many full-faced moons shall wane,
Lean-horned, before I come again
As one triumphant; when I find
In thee, all faith of womankind.
Nor would I have thee think, that thou
Had'st power thyself to keep this vow;
But having 'scaped temptation's shelf,
Know virtue taught thee, not thyself.

To Sir Clipsby Crewe

Since to the country first I came,
I have lost my former flame:
And, methinks, I not inherit,
As I did, my ravished spirit.
If I write a verse, or two,
'Tis with very much ado;
In regard I want that wine
Which should conjure up a line.
Yet, though now of Muse bereft,
I have still the manners left
For to thank you (noble Sir)
For those gifts you do confer
Upon him, who only can
Be in prose a grateful man.

Upon himself

I could never love indeed;
Never see mine own heart bleed:
Never crucify my life,
Or for widow, maid, or wife.

I could never seek to please
One, or many mistresses:
Never like their lips, to swear
Oil of roses still smelt there.

I could never break my sleep,
Fold mine arms, sob, sigh, or weep:
Never beg, or humbly woo
With oaths, and lies, (as others do.)

I could never walk alone;
Put a shirt of sackcloth on:
Never keep a fast, or pray
For good luck in love (that day.)

But have hitherto lived free,
As the air that circles me:
And kept credit with my heart,
Neither broke i'th' whole, or part.

Upon Jack and Jill. Epig.

When Jill complains to Jack for want of meat;
Jack kisses Jill, and bids her freely eat:
Jill says, of what? says Jack, on that sweet kiss,
Which full of nectar and ambrosia is,
The food of poets; so I thought says Jill,
That makes them look so lank, so ghost-like still.
Let poets feed on air, or what they will;
Let me feed full, till that I fart, says Jill.

To the Lady Crewe,
upon the death of her Child

Why, Madam, will ye longer weep,
When as your baby's lulled asleep?
And (pretty child) feels now no more
Those pains it lately felt before.
All now is silent; groans are fled:
Your child lies still, yet is not dead:
But rather like a flower hid here
To spring again another year.

To Phyllis to love, and live with him

Live, live with me, and thou shalt see
The pleasures I'll prepare for thee:
What sweets the country can afford
Shall bless thy bed, and bless thy board.
The soft sweet moss shall be thy bed,
With crawling woodbine over-spread:
By which the silver-shedding streams
Shall gently melt thee into dreams.
Thy clothing next, shall be a gown
Made of the fleeces' purest down.
The tongues of kids shall be thy meat;
Their milk thy drink; and thou shalt eat
The paste of filberts for thy bread
With cream of cowslips buttered:
Thy feasting-tables shall be hills
With daisies spread, and daffodils;
Where thou shalt sit, and red-breast by,
For meat, shall give thee melody.
I'll give thee chains and carcanets
Of primroses and violets.
A bag and bottle thou shalt have;
That richly wrought, and this as brave;
So that as either shall express
The wearer's no mean shepherdess.
At shearing-times, and yearly wakes,
When Themilis his pastime makes,
There thou shalt be; and be the wit,
Nay more, the feast, and grace of it.
On holidays, when virgins meet
To dance the heyes with nimble feet;
Thou shalt come forth, and then appear
The Queen of Roses for that year.
And having danced ('bove all the best)

Carry the garland from the rest.
In wicker baskets maids shall bring
To thee, (my dearest shepherdling)
The blushing apple, bashful pear,
And shame-faced plum, (all simp'ring there).
Walk in the groves, and thou shalt find
The name of Phyllis in the rind
Of every straight, and smooth-skin tree;
Where kissing that, I'll twice kiss thee.
To thee a sheep-hook I will send,
Be-pranked with ribands, to this end;
This, this alluring hook might be
Less for to catch a sheep, than me.
Thou shalt have possets, wassails fine,
Not made of ale, but spicèd wine,
To make thy maids and self free mirth,
All sitting near the glitt'ring hearth.
Thou shalt have ribands, roses, rings,
Gloves, garters, stockings, shoes, and strings
Of winning colours, that shall move
Others to lust, but me to love.
These (nay) and more, thine own shall be,
If thou wilt love, and live with me.

His content in the Country

Here, here I live with what my board,
Can with the smallest cost afford.
Though ne'r so mean the viands be,
They well content my Prew and me.
Or pea, or bean, or wort, or beet,
Whatever comes, content makes sweet:
Here we rejoice, because no rent
We pay for our poor tenement:
Wherein we rest, and never fear
The landlord, or the usurer.
The quarter-day does ne'r affright
Our peaceful slumbers in the night.
We eat our own, and batten more,
Because we feed on no man's score:
But pity those, whose flanks grow great,
Swelled with the lard of others' meat.
We bless our fortunes, when we see
Our own beloved privacy:
And like our living, where we're known
To very few, or else to none.

The Apparition of his Mistress
calling him to Elysium

Desunt nonnulla –
Come then, and like two doves with silv'ry wings,
Let our souls fly to th' shades, where ever springs
Sit smiling in the meads; where balm and oil,
Roses and cassia crown the untilled soil.
Where no disease reigns, or infection comes
To blast the air, but ambergris and gums.
This, that, and ev'ry thicket doth transpire
More sweet, than storax from the hallowed fire:
Where ev'ry tree a wealthy issue bears
Of fragrant apples, blushing plums, or pears:
And all the shrubs, with sparkling spangles, shew
Like morning sunshine tinselling the dew.
Here in green meadows sits eternal May,
Purfling the margents, while perpetual day
So double gilds the air, as that no night
Can ever rust th'enamel of the light.
Here, naked younglings, handsome striplings run
Their goals for virgins' kisses; which when done,
Then unto dancing forth the learnèd round
Commixed they meet, with endless roses crowned.
And here we'll sit on primrose-banks, and see
Love's chorus led by Cupid; and we'll be
Two loving followers too unto the grove,
Where poets sing the stories of our love.
There thou shalt hear divine Musæus sing
Of Hero, and Leander; then I'll bring
Thee to the stand, where honoured Homer reads
His Odysseys, and his high Iliads.
About whose throne the crowd of poets throng
To hear the incantation of his tongue:
To Linus, then to Pindar; and that done,

I'll bring thee Herrick to Anacreon,
Quaffing his full-crowned bowls of burning wine,
And in his raptures speaking lines of thine,
Like to his subject; and as his frantic
Looks, show him truly Bacchanalian like
Besmeared with grapes; welcome he shall thee thither,
Where both may rage, both drink and dance together.
Then stately Virgil, witty Ovid, by
Whom fair Corinna sits, and doth comply
With ivory wrists, his laureate head, and steeps
His eye in dew of kisses, while he sleeps.
Then soft Catullus, sharp-fanged Martial,
And towering Lucan, Horace, Juvenal,
And snaky Perseus, these, and those, whom rage
(Dropped for the jars of heaven) filled t'engage
All times unto their frenzies; thou shalt there
Behold them in a spacious theatre.
Among which glories, (crowned with sacred bays
And flatt'ring ivy) two recite their plays,
Beaumont and Fletcher, swans, to whom all ears
Listen, while they (like sirens in their spheres)
Sing their Evadne; and still more for thee
There yet remains to know, than thou can'st see
By glimm'ring of a fancy: do but come,
And there I'll show thee that capacious room
In which thy father Jonson now is placed,
As in a globe of radiant fire, and graced
To be in that orb crowned, that doth include
Those prophets of the former magnitude,
And he one chief; but hark, I hear the cock,
(The bell-man of the night) proclaim the clock
Of late struck one; and now I see the prime
Of day break from the pregnant east, 'tis time
I vanish; more I had to say;
But night determines here, away.

No luck in Love

I do love I know not what;
Sometimes this, & sometimes that:
All conditions I aim at.

But, as luckless, I have yet
Many shrewd disasters met,
To gain her whom I would get.

Therefore now I'll love no more,
As I've doted heretofore:
He who must be, shall be poor.

Upon Lucia

I asked my Lucia but a kiss;
And she with scorn denied me this:
Say then, how ill should I have sped,
Had I then asked her maidenhead?

The bad season makes the Poet sad

Dull to myself, and almost dead to these
My many fresh and fragrant mistresses:
Lost to all music now, since every thing
Puts on the semblance here of sorrowing.
Sick is the land to th' heart; and doth endure
More dangerous faintings by her desp'rate cure.
But if that golden age would come again,
And Charles here rule, as he before did reign;
If smooth and unperplexed the seasons were,
As when the sweet Maria lived here:
I should delight to have my curls half drowned
In Tyrian dews, and head with roses crowned.
And once more yet (ere I am laid out dead)
Knock at a star with my exalted head.

His charge to Julia at his death

Dearest of thousands, now the time draws near,
That with my lines, my life must full-stop here.
Cut off thy hairs; and let thy tears be shed
Over my turf, when I am buried.
Then for effusions, let none wanting be,
Or other rites that do belong to me;
As love shall help thee, when thou dost go hence
Unto thy everlasting residence.

The Country life,
to the honoured M. End. Porter,
Groom of the Bedchamber to His Maj.

Sweet country life, to such unknown,
Whose lives are others', not their own!
But serving courts, and cities, be
Less happy, less enjoying thee.
Thou never plough'st the ocean's foam
To seek, and bring rough pepper home:
Nor to the Eastern Ind dost rove
To bring from thence the scorchèd clove,
Nor, with the loss of thy loved rest,
Bring'st home the ingot from the West.
No, thy ambition's masterpiece
Flies no thought higher than a fleece:
Or how to pay thy hinds, and clear
All scores; and so to end the year:
But walk'st about thine own dear bounds,
Not envying others' larger grounds:
For well thou know'st, *'tis not th' extent*
Of land makes life, but sweet content.
When now the cock (the ploughman's horn)
Calls forth the lily-wristed morn;
Then to thy cornfields thou dost go,
Which though well soiled, yet thou dost know,
That the best compost for the lands
Is the wise master's feet, and hands.
There at the plough thou find'st thy team,
With a hind whistling there to them:
And cheer'st them up, by singing how
The kingdom's portion is the plough.
This done, then to th' enamelled meads
Thou go'st; and as thy foot there treads,
Thou see'st a present God-like power

Imprinted in each herb and flower:
And smell'st the breath of great-eyed kine,
Sweet as the blossoms of the vine.
Here thou behold'st thy large sleek neat
Unto the dewlaps up in meat:
And, as thou look'st, the wanton steer,
The heifer, cow, and ox draw near
To make a pleasing pastime there.
These seen, thou go'st to view thy flocks
Of sheep, (safe from the wolf and fox)
And find'st their bellies there as full
Of short sweet grass, as backs with wool.
And leav'st them (as they feed and fill)
A shepherd piping on a hill.
For sports, for pageantry, and plays,
Thou hast thy eves, and holy days:
On which the young men and maids meet,
To exercise their dancing feet:
Tripping the comely country round,
With daffodils and daisies crowned.
Thy wakes, thy quintels here thou hast,
Thy may-poles too with garlands graced:
Thy morris-dance; thy Whitsun ale;
Thy shearing-feast, which never fail.
Thy harvest-home; thy wassail bowl,
That's tossed up after fox i' th' hole.
Thy mummeries; thy twelve-tide kings
And queens; thy Christmas revellings:
Thy nut-brown mirth; thy russet wit;
And no man pays too dear for it.
To these, thou hast thy times to go
And trace the hare i'th' treacherous snow:
Thy witty wiles to draw, and get
The lark into the trammel net:
Thou hast thy cockrood, and thy glade

To take the precious pheasant made:
Thy lime-twigs, snares, and pit-falls then
To catch the pilf'ring birds, not men.
O happy life! if that their good
The husbandmen but understood!
Who all the day themselves do please,
And younglings, with such sports as these.
And, lying down, have nought t' affright
Sweet sleep, that makes more short the night.
                Cætera desunt –

What kind of Mistress he would have

Be the mistress of my choice,
Clean in manners, clear in voice:
Be she witty, more than wise;
Pure enough, though not precise:
Be she showing in her dress,
Like a civil wilderness;
That the curious may detect
Order in a sweet neglect:
Be she rolling in her eye,
Tempting all the passers-by:
And each ringlet of her hair,
An enchantment, or a snare,
For to catch the lookers-on;
But herself held fast by none.
Let her Lucrece all day be,
Thais in the night, to me.
Be she such, as neither will
Famish me, nor overfill.

A Paranetical, or Advisive Verse
to his Friend, Mr John Wicks

Is this a life, to break thy sleep?
To rise as soon as day doth peep?
To tire thy patient ox or ass
By noon, and let thy good days pass,
Not knowing this, that Jove decrees
Some mirth, t'adulce man's miseries?
No; 'tis a life, to have thine oil,
Without extortion, from thy soil:
Thy faithful fields to yield thee grain,
Although with some, yet little pain:
To have thy mind, and nuptial bed,
With fears, and cares uncumbered:
A pleasing wife, that by thy side
Lies softly panting like a bride.
This is to live, and to endear
Those minutes, time has lent us here.
Then, while fates suffer, live thou free,
(As is that air that circles thee)
And crown thy temples too, and let
Thy servant, not thy own self, sweat,
To strut thy barns with sheaves of wheat.
Time steals away like to a stream,
And we glide hence away with them.
No sound recalls the hours once fled,
Or roses, being withered:
Nor us (my friend) when we are lost,
Like to a dew, or melted frost.
Then live we mirthful, while we should,
And turn the iron age to gold.
Let's feast, and frolic, sing, and play,
And thus less last, than live our day.
Whose life with care is overcast,

That man's not said to live, but last:
Nor is't a life, seven years to tell,
But for to live that half seven well:
And that we'll do; as men, who know,
Some few sands spent, we hence must go,
Both to be blended in the urn,
From whence there's never a return.

To Anthea

Come Anthea, know thou this,
Love at no time idle is;
Let's be doing, though we play
But at push-pin (half the day:)
Chains of sweet bents let us make,
Captive one, or both, to take:
In which bondage we will lie,
Souls transfusing thus, and die.

Stool-ball

At stool-ball, Lucia, let us play,
 For sugar-cakes and wine;
Or for a tansy let us pay,
 The loss or thine, or mine.

If thou, my dear, a winner be
 At trundling of the ball,
The wager thou shalt have, and me,
 And my misfortunes all.

But if (my sweetest) I shall get,
 Then I desire but this;
That likewise I may pay the bet,
 And have for all a kiss.

To Sappho

Let us now take time, and play,
Love, and live here while we may;
Drink rich wine; and make good cheer,
While we have our being here:
For, once dead, and laid i'th grave,
No return from thence we have.

On Poet Prat, Epigr.

Prat he writes satires; but herein's the fault,
In no one satire there's a mite of salt.

His return to London

From the dull confines of the drooping West,
To see the day spring from the pregnant East,
Ravished in spirit, I come, nay more, I fly
To thee, blest place of my nativity!
Thus, thus with hallowed foot I touch the ground,
With thousand blessings by thy fortune crowned.
O fruitful genius! that bestowest here
An everlasting plenty, year by year.
O place! O people! Manners! framed to please
All nations, customs, kindreds, languages!
I am a free-born Roman; suffer, then,
That I amongst you live a citizen.
London my home is: though by hard fate sent
Into a long and irksome banishment;
Yet since called back; henceforward let me be,
O native country, repossessed by thee!
For, rather then I'll to the West return,
I'll beg of thee first here to have mine urn.
Weak I am grown, and must in short time fall;
Give thou my sacred relics burial.

Upon Julia's sweat

Would ye oil of blossoms get?
Take it from my Julia's sweat:
Oil of lilies, and of spike,
From her moisture take the like:
Let her breathe, or let her blow,
All rich spices thence will flow.

Proof to no purpose

You see this gentle stream, that glides,
Shoved on, by quick succeeding tides:
Try if this sober stream you can
Follow to th' wilder ocean:
And see, if there it keeps unspent
In that congesting element.
Next, from that world of waters, then
By pores and caverns back again
Induced that inadultrate same
Streame to the spring from whence it came.
This with a wonder when ye do,
As easy, and else easier too:
Then may ye recollect the grains
Of my particular remains;
After a thousand lusters hurled,
By ruffling winds, about the world.

Upon Lucia dabbled in the dew

My Lucia in the dew did go,
And prettily bedabbled so,
Her clothes held up, she showed withall
Her decent legs, clean, long and small.
I followed after to descry
Part of the nak'd sincerity;
But still the envious scene between
Denied the mask I would have seen.

To Sir John Berkeley, Governor of Exeter

Stand forth, brave man, since fate has made thee here
The Hector over agèd Exeter;
Who for a long sad time has weeping stood,
Like a poor lady lost in widowhood:
But fears not now to see her safety sold
(As other towns and cities were) for gold,
By those ignoble births, which shame the stem
That gave progermination unto them:
Whose restless ghosts shall hear their children sing,
Our sires betrayed their country and their king.
True, if this city seven times rounded was
With rock, and seven times circumflanked with brass,
Yet if thou wert not, Berkeley, loyal proof,
The senators down tumbling with the roof,
Would into praised (but pitied) ruins fall,
Leaving no show, where stood the capitol.
But thou art just and itchless, and dost please
Thy genius with two strength'ning buttresses,
Faith, and affection: which will never slip
To weaken this thy great dictatorship.

The Invitation

To sup with thee thou did'st me home invite;
And mad'st a promise that mine appetite
Should meet and tire, on such lautitious meat,
The like not Heliogabalus did eat:
And richer wine would'st give to me (thy guest)
Than Roman Sylla poured out at his feast.
I came; ('tis true) and looked for fowl of price,
The bastard phoenix; bird of paradise;
And for no less than aromatic wine
Of maiden's-blush, commixed with jessamine.
Clean was the hearth, the mantle larded jet;
Which wanting lar, and smoke, hung weeping wet;
At last, i'th' noon of winter, did appear
A ragg'd-sous'd-neat's-foot with sick vinegar:
And in a burnished flagonet stood by
Beer small as comfort, dead as charity.
At which amazed, and pond'ring on the food,
How cold it was, and how it chilled my blood;
I cursed the master, and I damned the souse,
And swore I'd got the ague of the house.
Well, when to eat thou dost me next desire,
I'll bring a fever, since thou keep'st no fire.

To Anthea

Anthea I am going hence
With some small stock of innocence:
But yet those blessèd gates I see
Withstanding entrance unto me.
To pray for me do thou begin,
The porter then will let me in.

To M. Henry Lawes,
the excellent Composer of his Lyrics

Touch but thy lyre (my Harry) and I hear
From thee some raptures of the rare Gotier.
Then if thy voice commingle with the string
I hear in thee rare Lanier to sing;
Or curious Wilson: tell me, canst thou be
Less than Apollo, that usurp'st such three?
Three, unto whom the whole world give applause;
Yet their three praises, praise but one; that's Lawes.

Julia's Churching, or Purification

Put on thy holy fillitings, and so
To th' temple with the sober midwife go.
Attended thus (in a most solemn wise)
By those who serve the childbed mysteries.
Burn first thine incense; next, when as thou see'st
The candid stole thrown o're the pious priest;
With reverend curtseys come, and to him bring
Thy free (and not decurted) offering.
All rites well ended, with fair auspice come
(As to the breaking of a bride-cake) home:
Where ceremonious Hymen shall for thee
Provide a second epithalamy.
She who keeps chastely to her husband's side
Is not for one, but every night his bride:
And stealing still with love, and fear to bed,
Brings him not one, but many a maidenhead.

Upon M. William Lawes, the rare Musician

Should I not put on blacks, when each one here
Comes with his cypress, and devotes a tear?
Should I not grieve (my Lawes) when every lute,
Viol, and voice, is (by thy loss) struck mute?
Thy loss brave man! whose numbers have been hurled,
And no less praised, than spread throughout the world.
Some have thee called Amphion; some of us,
Named thee Terpander, or sweet Orpheus:
Some this, some that, but all in this agree,
Music had both her birth, and death with thee.

To his peculiar friend M. Jo: Wicks

Since shed or cottage I have none,
I sing the more, that thou hast one;
To whose glad threshold, and free door
I may a poet come, though poor;
And eat with thee a savoury bit,
Paying but common thanks for it.
Yet should I chance, (my Wicks) to see
An over-leaven look in thee,
To sour the bread, and turn the beer
To an exalted vinegar;
Or shouldst thou prize me as a dish
Of thrice-boiled worts, or third day's fish;
I'd rather hungry go and come,
Than to thy house be burdensome;
Yet, in my depth of grief, I'd be
One that should drop his beads for thee.

To Julia

Help me, Julia, for to pray,
Matins sing, or matins say:
This I know, the fiend will fly
Far away, if thou beest by.
Bring the holy water hither;
Let us wash, and pray together:
When our beads are thus united,
Then the foe will fly affrighted.

His Covenant or Protestation to Julia

Why dost thou wound, & break my heart?
As if we should for ever part?
Hast thou not heard an oath from me,
After a day, or two, or three,
I would come back and live with thee?
Take, if thou dost distrust that vow;
This second protestation now.
Upon thy cheek that spangled tear,
Which sits as dew of roses there:
That tear shall scarce be dried before
I'll kiss the threshold of thy door.
Then weep not sweet; but thus much know,
I'm half returned before I go.

His Last Request to Julia

I have been wanton, and too bold I fear,
To chafe o're-much the virgin's cheek or ear:
Beg for my pardon Julia; *he doth win*
Grace with the gods, who's sorry for his sin.
That done, my Julia, dearest Julia, come,
And go with me to choose my burial room:
My fates are ended; when thy Herrick dies,
Clasp thou his book, then close thou up his eyes.

The Pillar of Fame

Fame's pillar here, at last, we set,
Outduring marble, brass, or jet,
Charmed and enchanted so,
As to withstand the blow
Of   overthrow;
Nor shall the seas,
Or   outrages
Of storms o'rebear
What we up-rear,
Tho' kingdoms fall,
This pillar never shall
Decline or waste at all;
But stand for ever by his own
Firm and well-fixed foundation.

His Ejaculation to God

My God! look on me with thine eye
Of pity, not of scrutiny;
For if thou dost, thou then shalt see
Nothing but loathsome sores in me.
O then! for mercy's sake, behold
These my eruptions manifold;
And heal me with thy look, or touch:
But if thou wilt not deign so much,
Because I'm odious in thy sight,
Speak but the word, and cure me quite.

To God, on his Sickness

What though my harp, and viol be
Both hung upon the willow tree?
What though my bed be now my grave,
And for my house I darkness have?
What though my healthful days are fled,
And I lie numbered with the dead?
Yet I have hope, by Thy great power,
To spring; though now a withered flower.

A Thanksgiving to God, for his House

Lord, Thou hast given me a cell
    Wherein to dwell;
A little house, whose humble roof
    Is weather-proof;
Under the spars of which I lie
    Both soft, and dry;
Where Thou, my chamber for to ward
    Hast set a guard
Of harmless thoughts, to watch and keep
    Me, while I sleep.
Low is my porch, as is my fate,
    Both void of state;
And yet the threshold of my door
    Is worn by th' poor,
Who thither come, and freely get
    Good words, or meat:
Like as my parlour, so my hall
    And kitchen's small:
A little buttery, and therein
    A little bin,
Which keeps my little loaf of bread
    Unchipped, unflea'd:
Some brittle sticks of thorn or briar
    Make me a fire,
Close by whose living coal I sit,
    And glow like it.
Lord, I confess too, when I dine,
    The pulse is Thine,
And all those other bits, that be
    There placed by Thee;
The worts, the purslain, and the mess
    Of watercress,
Which of thy kindness Thou hast sent;

And my content
Makes those, and my beloved beet,
　　　To be more sweet.
'Tis Thou that crown'st my glittering hearth
　　　With guiltless mirth;
And giv'st me wassail bowls to drink,
　　　Spiced to the brink.
Lord, 'tis Thy plenty-dropping hand,
　　　That soils my land;
And giv'st me, for my bushel sown,
　　　Twice ten for one:
Thou mak'st my teeming hen to lay
　　　Her egg each day:
Besides my healthful ewes to bear
　　　Me twins each year:
The while the conduits of my kine
　　　Run cream, (for wine.)
All these, and better Thou dost send
　　　Me, to this end,
That I should render, for my part,
　　　A thankful heart;
Which, fired with incense, I resign,
　　　As wholly Thine;
But the acceptance, that must be,
　　　My Christ, by Thee.

To his Ever-loving God

Can I not come to Thee, my God, for these
So very many meeting hindrances,
That slack my pace; but yet not make me stay?
Who slowly goes, rids (in the end) his way.
Clear Thou my paths, or shorten Thou my miles,
Remove the bars, or lift me o're the stiles:
Since rough the way is, help me when I call,
And take me up; or else prevent the fall.
I kenn my home; and it affords some ease,
To see far off the smoking villages.
Fain would I rest; yet covet not to die,
For fear of future-biting penury:
No, no, (my God) Thou know'st my wishes be
To leave this life, not loving it, but Thee.

To His Sweet Saviour

Night hath no wings, to him that cannot sleep;
And time seems then, not for to fly, but creep;
Slowly her chariot drives, as if that she
Had broke her wheel, or cracked her axletree.
Just so it is with me, who list'ning, pray
The winds, to blow the tedious night away;
That I might see the cheerful peeping day.
Sick is my heart; O Saviour! do Thou please
To make my bed soft in my sicknesses:
Lighten my candle, so that I beneath
Sleep not for ever in the vaults of death:
Let me Thy voice betimes i'th' morning hear;
Call, and I'll come; say Thou the when, and where:
Draw me, but first, and after Thee I'll run,
And make no one stop, till my race be done.

Mr Robert Herrick his farewell unto Poetry

I have beheld two lovers in a night
(Hatched o're with moonshine, from their stolen delight)
When this to that, and that, to this, had given
A kiss to such a jewel of the heaven:
Or while that each from other's breath did drink
Healths to the rose, the violet, or pink,
Called on the sudden by the jealous mother,
Some stricter mistress or suspicious other
Urging divorcement (worse than death to this)
By the soon jingling of some sleepy keys,
Part with a hasty kiss; and in that show
How stay they would, yet forced they are to go.
Even such are we; and in our parting, do
No otherwise than as those former two
Natures, like ours, we who have spent our time
Both from the morning to the evening chime;
Nay tell the bell-man of the night had told
Past noon of night, yet were the hours not old
Nor dulled with iron sleeps; but have out-worn
The fresh and fairest flourish of the morn
With flame, and rapture; drinking to the odd
Number of nine, which makes us full with God,
And in that mystic frenzy, we have hurled
(As with a tempest) nature through the world
And in a whirlwind twirled her home, aghast
At that which in her ecstasy had passed;
Thus crowned with rose-buds, sack, thou mad'st me fly
Like firedrakes, yet didst me no harm thereby.
O thou almighty nature, who didst give
True heat, wherewith humanity doth live
Beyond its stinted circle; giving food
(White fame) and resurrection to the good,
Soaring them up, 'bove ruin, till the doom

(The general April of the world) doth come,
That makes all equal. Many thousands should
(Wert not for thee) have crumbled into mould,
And with their cearecloth̄es rotted, not to show
Whether the world such spirits had or no,
Whereas by thee, those, and a million since
Nor fate, nor envy, can their fames convince,
Homer, Musaeus, Ovid, Maro, more
Of those god-full prophets long before
Hold their eternal fires; and ours of late
(Thy mercy helping) shall resist strong fate
Nor stoop to th' centre, but survive as long
As fame or rumour, hath or trump or tongue.
But unto me, be only hoarse, since now
(Heaven and my soul bear record of my vow)
I, my desires screw from thee, and direct
Them and my thoughts to that sublimed respect
And conscience unto priesthood, 'tis not need
(The scarecrow unto mankind) that doth breed
Wiser conclusions in me, since I know
I've more to bear my charge, than way to go,
Or had I not, I'd stop the spreading itch
Of craving more: so in conceit be rich.
But 'tis the God of nature, who intends
And shapes my function, for more glorious ends:
Guess, so depart; yet stay a while to see
The lines of sorrow, that lie drawn in me
In speech, in picture; no otherwise than when
(Judgement and death, denounced 'gainst guilty men)
Each takes a weeping farewell, racked in mind
Wth joys before, and pleasures left behind:
Shaking the head, whilst each, to each doth mourn,
With thought they go, whence they must ne'r return.
So with like looks, as once the minstrel

Cast, leading his Eurydice through hell,
I stricke thy loves, and greedily pursue
Thee, with mine eyes, or in, or out, of view.
So looked the Grecian orator when sent
From's native country, into banishment,
Throwing his eyeballs backward, to survey
The smoke of his beloved Attica,
So Tully looked, when from the breasts of Rome
The sad soul went, not with his love, but doom;
Shooting his eye-darts 'gainst it, to surprise
It, or to draw the city to his eyes.
Such is my parting with thee; and to prove
There was not varnish (only) in my love
But substance, too! receive this pearly tear
Frozen with grief; and place it in thine ear,
Then part in name of peace; & softly on
With numerous feet to hoofy Helicon,
And when thou art upon that forkèd hill
Amongst the thrice three sacred virgins, fill
A full brimmed bowl of fury and of rage
And quaff it to the prophets of our age;
When drunk with rapture; curse the blind & lame
Base ballad-mongers, who usurp thy name
And foul thy altar, charm some into frogs,
Some to be rats, and others to be hogs:
Into the loathsomst shapes, thou canst devise
To make fools hate them, only by disguise;
Thus with a kiss of warmth, and love, I part
Not so, but that some relic in my heart
Shall stand for ever, though I do address
Chiefly myself to what I must profess:
Know yet, (rare soul,) when my diviner Muse
Shall want a handmaid, (as she oft will use)
Be ready, thou in me, to wait upon her
Though as a servant, yet a maid of honour.

The Crown of duty is our duty; well
Doing's, the fruit of doing well, farewell.

Finis Mr Robt Herrick

[*Epitaph on the Tomb of Sir Edward Giles and his wife in the South Aisle of Dean Prior Church.*]

No trust to metals nor to marbles, when
These have their fate, and wear away as men;
Times, titles, trophies, may be lost and spent;
But virtue rears the eternal monument.
What more than these can tombs or tombstones pay?
But here's the sunset of a tedious day:
These two asleep are: I'll but be undressed
And so to bed: pray wish us all good rest.

Notes to the Poems

The Argument of his Book (p.13)
July-flowers: gilly-flowers; pinks.

hock-cart: The last cart of grain from the harvest-field. The cart's arrival signalled the beginning of the Harvest Home feast.

wassail: hot, spiced punch. In Herrick's time it is likely to have been made with beer.

wakes: village festivals.

ambergris: An intestinal secretion of the sperm-whale, used as an odorant in perfumes. In Renaissance times, it was also dried and moulded into jewellery, especially beads.

Mab: Queen of the fairies

fairy-king: i.e. Oberon.

To his Mistresses (p.15)
Æson: father of Jason (of the Argonauts) who was rejuvenated by Medea, Jason's enchantress wife. The tale is recounted in Ovid's *Metamorphoses*.

To Anthea (p.15)
holy filletings: also spelled 'fillitings' – the cloths that make up a woman's veil, worn when attending church.

Discontents in Devon (p.16)
numbers: poems. Herrick's poems on sacred themes were gathered under the title *His Noble Numbers* in 1648, as part of his collected poems, *Hesperides*.

To Anthea (p.17)
Holy oak: the oak under which the minister read the Gospel in the procession around the parish boundaries in Rogation week (i.e. the week in which Ascension Day was celebrated). Also connected with Saint Boniface, the 7th century saint born in Crediton, Devon (some 20 miles from Herrick's village of Dean Prior), who felled the holy oak tree dedicated to Thor in what is today the state of Hesse in Germany. Boniface called upon Thor to strike him down if he cut down the holy tree. When nothing happened, the people converted to Christianity. Boniface built a chapel from the wood of the felled oak.

Gospel-tree: the pagan British tradition of celebrating rituals in the shade of an oak tree continued after the introduction of Christianity, whence its English nickname, 'the prayer tree' or 'gospel tree'.

Dean Bourn, a rude River in Devon... (p.19)

Title: Dean Bourn is a small river that runs through Dean Prior, some 10 minutes' walk from Herrick's church.

warty: some copies of *Hesperides* have *watry*, i.e. watery, which is the logical reading, but I suspect that the punning 'warty' which appears in the facsimile of the British Library's copy to be correct.

currish: ignoble, bad-natured.

salvages: savages

A Country life... (p.20-24)

brass: money.

cocker: pamper, spoil.

tearcely: tersely, purely.

neat: dainty.

spirting-salt: in an ode by Horace, 'duteous cake and spirting salt' are listed as lowly offerings to the gods.

Chanticleer: a proud rooster and protagonist of the fable 'Chanticleer and the Fox'. The story is related in Chaucer's 'The Nun's Priest's Tale', part of *The Canterbury Tales*.

lars: i.e. *lares* – the (Roman) household gods.

cates: delicacies, luxury foods.

larded fare: either meat covered with lard, or meat in which strips of fat or bacon had been inserted before cooking.

colworts: cabbages.

conning: studying, learning.

size: a ration of food.

kitling: kitten.

The frozen Zone (p.24)

congelation: lit. congealing. Here, freezing.

Upon Cuffe. Epig (p. 25)

briefs: Letters patent issued by the monarch as Governor of the Church of England, licensing a collection in churches for a specific object of charity. (*OED*).

The Hour-glass (p.25)
humour: moisture.

His farewell to Sack (p.26-27)
sack: a wine imported from Spain or the Canaries. In *The English Housewife* (1683) Gervase Markham says: "Your best Sackes are of Seres [modern Jerez; in late 15th Century Spanish, Xeres] in Spain, your smaller of Galicia or Portugal: your strong Sackes are of the islands of the Canaries." Herrick refers to "Canary sack" in his poem 'Welcome to Sack' (see. pp.44-46) and thus it may be safely assumed that he refers to the Spanish wine, which was cheap in his day. Shakespeare's Falstaff referred to "Sherris-sack" (i.e. Jerez sack) in *Henry IV*, Part 2. The word probably derives from the Spanish *saca* (withdrawal/extract, i.e. from the ageing barrels); shipments of wine were known as *sacas*, referred to thus on trade documents. French *sec* (dry) is another possible source.
shagg'd: rough-haired.
mystic fan: from the first of Virgil's *Georgics* – the mystic fan of Iacchus was a sieve on the threshing-floor.
Castalian sisters: i.e. the Muses. The Castalian spring, located in a cave near Delphi, was an obligatory port of call for supplicants at the Oracle, where they would wash their hair. The spring became a symbol of poetic inspiration.
Horace: Roman poet, Quintus Horatius Flaccus (65–8BC).
Anacreon: Greek lyric poet from the early 6th century BC. One of the canonical nine lyric poets of later tradition (with Alcman, Sappho, Alcaeus, Stesichorus, Ibycus, Simonides, Pindar and Bacchylides).
Phoebean: from *phoebus* (bright), the standard epithet for the god Apollo.
Thespian spring: a city in Greece, not far from Delphi and next to Mount Helicon, home of two springs sacred to the Muses.
numbers: verses.
cedar: cedar oil, used for the preservation of manuscripts.

The suspicion upon his over-much familiarity... (p.28-29)
sprightful: sprightly, full of life.

Upon the Bishop of Lincoln's Imprisonment (p.29)

Title: The Bishop was John Williams (1582-1650), imprisoned in the Tower of London for political reasons from 1636 to 1640.

Dissuasions from Idleness (p.30)

Cynthius: Greek god of light and music. A variation of Apollo.

An Epithalamy to Sir Thomas Southwell and His Lady (p.31-37)

epithalamy: Epithalamium, or wedding song.

Hymen: Greek God of marriage

Domiduca: a Roman goddess who escorted children safely home.

turtles: turtledoves

Juno: goddess of marriage and both sister and wife to Jupiter, ruler of the gods.

Zephyrus: god of the West Wind.

reaks: pranks.

fillets: veils, or ribbons.

reak: prank, or trick.

Barley-break: a country game, played by three mixed pairs, each stationed in their own base, the three bases being next to each other. The couple in the middle, their base being known as Hell or Prison, had to catch the other two couples, who were permitted to 'break' when chased. If they were overtaken, or caught, they were condemned to 'Hell'.

Panchaia: legendary land of spices mentioned by Virgil.

To Jos., Bishop of Exeter (p.40)

Title: Joseph Hall was born at Ashby-de-la-Zouch and educated at Emmanuel College, Cambridge, where he was one of the 'University wits'. He published his *Virgidemiarum*, six books of satires, in 1597 and 1598. These verse satires were amongst the earliest English satires on classical models.

Hall was appointed chaplain to Prince Henry in 1608, and was made Dean of Worcester by James I. He was made Bishop of Exeter in 1627, and of Norwich in 1641.

In 1641, Hall published *Episcopacy by Divine Right, Asserted by J. H.*, an attack on *Smectymnus* (1641), a pamphlet against episcopacy. This brought him into conflict with Milton. In 1642, Hall was among 13 bishops imprisoned by Parliament.

His cathedral was desecrated in the Civil War, and Hall himself was evicted from his palace in 1647. Reduced to penury, he nonetheless survived until 1656.

Excathedrated: condemned *ex cathedra*, i.e. by the Bishop.

To the Detractor (p.40)
fellon: a sore, usually on the finger.
whitflaw: or whitlow, a lesion on the finger.

Corinna's going a-Maying (p.41-3)
Aurora: Roman goddess of the dawn.
Flora: Roman goddess of flowers.
fetch in May: to gather the white hawthorn flowers, and thus to celebrate the coming of Spring.
beads: prayers.
left to dream: ceased dreaming.
green-gown: tumble on the grass.

The Welcome to Sack (p.44-46)
Osiris: here, the Sun [Herrick's own note].
Ithaca: home of Odysseus.
sea-scourged merchant: i.e. Odysseus.
Iphyclus: One of the Argonauts, and son of King Phylacus of Phylace. Iphiclus was reputed to be one of the fastest runners in the world, so much so that he could run on the tips of growing corn without bending the stalks.
Isis: here, the Moon [Herrick's own note].
Cassius: one of Brutus' co-conspirators in the assassination of Julius Caesar. He drank only water.
Cato: Cato the Elder (234-149 BC), considered the first great Roman prose-writer, and the author of a manual on farming, *De agricultura*, which, among other things, covers vineyards and the making of wine.
Jove's son: Hercules.
Tyrinthian: Hercules. Ovid referred to him as the Tyrinthian in the *Fasti*.
Triumvir: Mark Antony, one of the Second Triumvirate of Rome, with Octavian and Lepidus.
Daphne: a river nymph with whom Apollo fell in love, following a prank by Cupid. Daphne despised the very idea of love and

spurned all advances. She fled from the amorous Apollo, who chased her to the point at which she, exhausted, was transformed into a laurel tree. Apollo took leaves from the tree to wear on his head, and in return said that the laurel tree would ever be green, echoing his own eternal youth.

To live merrily, and to trust to Good Verses (p.48-49)

Arabian dew: fragrant oil.

uncontrolled brow: uninhibited look.

retorted: slicked back.

pledge: toast.

terce: burnished.

Virgil, Ovid, Catullus, Propertius, Tibullus: great poets of ancient Rome.

thyrse: thyrsus – a staff tipped with pine-cone and woven round with ivy, carried by the god Bacchus.

Lethe: in Greek mythology one of the rivers of Hades, drinking from the waters of which would lead to complete forgetfulness.

Upon Julia's breasts (p.52)

circummortal: i.e. more than mortal, but also hinting through the prefix circum (*Latin* 'around') at circularity, roundness.

via lactea: *Latin*, Milky Way

The Hock-cart, or Harvest home... (p.54-55)

Title: Mildmay Fane, 2nd Earl of Westmorland (1602-1666) was a poet and MP for Peterborough. A suporter of the royalist cause, he was imprisoned briefly by the Commonweath forces, but then retired to his estate in Northamptonshire.

hock-cart: see first note on page 104.

maukin: a cloth; also a mop made of cloths attached to a pole, and a scarecrow.

prank: decorate.

wakes: village festivals.

ambergris: see fourth note on p.104.

frumenty: a dish of boiled grain, sweetened with sugar and spices.

fane: i.e. fan, used in winnowing grain. Also the surname of the poem's dedicatee: Mildmay Fane.

fats: vats, or barrels, for storing grain.

neat: cattle

harrow: tool used in the cultivation of the surface of the soil (as distinct from the plough, which digs much deeper).

Upon the death of his Sparrow. An Elegy (p.56)

Phil: i.e. Philip or Phip – a pet name for a sparrow.

Lesbia: the lover to whom Catullus addressed a number of his poems. It is unclear whether Lesbia was a real person, but her name carries echoes of Lesbos, home of the poet Sappho.

Virgil's gnat: one of Virgil's minor poems is 'Culex', usually translated as 'The Gnat', in which the insect relates the story of its travels to a shepherd.

To Virgins (p.60)

Rosamond: Rosamond (de) Clifford, a.k.a. Rosamond the Fair, lover of Henry II, forced by Eleanor of Aquitaine, Henry's Queen, to commit suicide at the palace of Woodstock. Her only protection had been labythinthine access to the house, and a single armed guard.

Danae: Danaë was the daughter of King Acrisius of Argos, who, saddened by the fact that he had no male issue, asked an oracle if this would change. He was told that he would be killed by his daughter's child. As his daughter was childless, Acrisius had her locked up in a cave, but she was visited by Zeus, by whom she bore Perseus. Perseus was eventually to kill Acrisius in an accident at the Games of Larissa, thus fulfilling the prophecy.

Hesperides: in Greek mythology, nymphs who tend a beautiful garden in a far-off corner of the world, to the west. Greek geographers, such as Strabo, located the garden in what is now southern Spain, or north Africa. The garden was an orchard, created by Hera, wife of Zeus, where the golden apples grew that give immortality. Also, the title of Herrick's collected poems, published in 1648.

babies in your eyes: most likely refers to the Latin *pupilla* (little girl), English "pupil," for the central spot of the eye. Although it refers to the reflection of the onlooker in the eyes of the one beheld, the phrase "to look babies in the eyes" means to gaze amorously.

The Entertainment; or, Porch-verse, at the Marriage of Mr. Henry Northly and the Most Witty Mrs. Lettice Yard (p.61)

Title: Henry Northly and Lettice Yard were parishioners of Herrick's at Dean Prior, Lettice Yard being the great-niece of Sir Edward Giles of Dean Court, the nearby manor house.

white: favourable.

To the most fair and lovely Mistress Anne Soame... (p.62)

jessamine: a.k.a. false jasmine (*Gelsemium sempervirens*).

factors: workers.

respasses: raspberries.

warden: an old variety of baking pear (OED).

pomander: ball of perfumes carried – usually around the neck – as a ward against infection as well as bad smells.

Upon M. Ben Jonson. Epig. (p.63)

Title: Ben Jonson was a great English poet and dramatist of the late Elizabethan and early Jacobean period. Herrick had known him, and was counted amongst his poetic followers.

sock; buskin: types of footwear worn by actors of comedy and tragedy, respectively, and thus symbols thereof.

cirque: circle or circus, i.e. theatre.

The Alchemist: Jonson's most famous comedy (1610).

To his Book (p. 64)

close-stools: commodes.

superlast: outlive.

Upon Parson Beanes (p.64)

hollows: shouts, 'hollers'.

To Groves (p.67)

fillets: ribbons.

Phyllis: a Thracian princess, daughter of Lycurgus, who hanged herself for love of her departed husband, Demophoön, son of Theseus. The story appears in Ovid's *Heroides*.

Iphis: a Cypriot youth who hanged himself for love of Anaxarete, who had spurned his advances. According to Ovid, Aphrodite turned Anaxarete to stone for her cold-heartedness.

To the right Honourable Mildmay, Earl of Westmorland (p.68)
Title: See p.109 for more on the Earl.
sibyls: prophetesses of Greek mythology. The Sibyl of Cumae, according to Virgil, would write her prophecies on leaves and place them outside her cave, where the wind would blow them away.
numbers: verses.

carcanet: necklace.
Belus' eye: onyx — "...that stone which men call Belus' eye, that is white and hath within it a black apple, the midst whereof a man shall see to glitter like gold." (Pliny's *History of the World*, translated by Philemon Holland, London 1601.)
Horace: Roman poet, Quintus Horatius Flaccus (65–8BC).

The parting Verse or charge to his supposed Wife... (p.69-71)
Queen of Ithaca: Penelope, wife of Odysseus.
incubi: demons in male form that were thought in medieval times to force themselves sexually upon sleeping women.
Lucrece: In 509 BC, Sextus Tarquinius, son of Tarquin, the King of Rome, raped Lucretia (Lucrece), wife of Collatinus, one of the King's retainers. Lucrece then committed suicide, and her body was paraded in the Forum by the King's nephew. This incited a revolt against the Tarquins, the banishment of the royal family, and the founding of the Roman republic. The sources for the story are Ovid's *Fasti* and Livy's history of Rome, *Ab urbe condita* (From the Founding of the City), but more recently for Herrick, also in Shakespeare's narrative poem *The Rape of Lucrece* (1597).
Cyane: a naiad (water-nymph) of Syracuse in Sicily, who witnessed the abduction of Persephone by Hades and then dissolved in grief.
Medullina: Livia Medullina Camilla, second fiancée of the Emperor Claudius. According to Suetonius, she fell ill and died on the day of her wedding to Claudius.
compression: embrace.

To Sir Clipsby Crewe (p.71)
Title: Crewe was a fellow student of Herrick's at St John's College, Cambridge. They were to remain lifelong friends.

To Phyllis, to love and live with him (p.74-5)
filberts: a type of hazelnut.
carcanets: necklaces.
the heyes: a winding, country dance.
be-pranked: decorated.
posset: a hot milk drink, curdled with wine or ale, with added spices.
wassail: hot, spiced punch. In Herrick's time it is likely to have been made with beer.

His content in the Country (page 76)
viands: victuals, food.
Prew: Herrick's housemaid, Prudence Baldwin.
batten: thrive.
score: indebtedness.

The Apparition of his Mistress calling him to Elysium (p.77-8)
Desunt nonnulla: Latin: 'something is missing', implying that the poem has been cut before this point, and a phrase which also famously appears in Marlowe's 'Hero and Leander'.
cassia: a spice, related to cinnamon, with variants native to the Middle East, India and Indonesia.
storax: a resin exuded by the sweetgum, sometimes used in incense or perfumes.
purfling: (also *purfle*) a decorated border on clothing, furniture or musical instruments.
Margents: margins or borders.
Musaeus: mythical first poet of ancient Greece; pupil or son of Orpheus.
Hero and Leander: Hero was a priestess of Aphrodite, living in a tower in Sestos on the Hellespont (the Bosporus); her lover Leander was a young man from Abydos, on the other side of the strait, who would swim the Hellespont every night to be with her, guided by means of a lamp placed by Hero at the top of the tower. One stormy winter's night, however, the light was extinguished and Leander drowned. Hero threw herself from the tower in despair. Both Ovid and Musaeus covered the subject, as did Christopher Marlowe (1564-1593), in his eponymous long poem.

Linus: probably the Linus who was the son of Apollo and Terpsichore, and who taught music to both Orpheus and Heracles (the Greek form of *Hercules*). Heracles killed him with his own lyre after Linus had criticised Heracles for his errors while playing.

Pindar: Pindaros (522–443 BC), one of the greatest lyric poets of ancient Greece.

Corinna: 6th-century BC Greek poet, reputedly the teacher of Pindar.

Anacreon: Greek lyric poet from the early 6th century BC. One of the canonical nine lyric poets of later tradition.

Bacchanalia: wild festivals of the god Bacchus (god of wine).

Catullus, Lucan, Horace, Juvenal, Martial: Roman poets

Beaumont and Fletcher: (1584-1616 & 1579-1625) dramatists of the late Eliabethan and early Jacobean period, and contemporaries of Jonson.

Evadne: character in the *The Maid's Tragedy* (1610) by Beaumont & Fletcher, who is to be married to Amintor in a sham marriage to cover up the King's own continuing liaison with her.

The bad season makes the Poet sad (p.80)

Charles: Charles I, King of England.

Maria: Henrietta Maria, his Queen.

Tyrian dews: purple or crimson dyes, for which the city of Tyre was famous.

The Country life, to the honoured M. End. Porter... (p.81-3)

Title: Endymion Porter (1587-1649) – son of an important landowner in Gloucestershire, he was brought up by his grandparents in Spain. After returning to England, he was employed by the Duke of Buckingham and then joined the royal court and accompanied King Charles on a visit to Madrid. He took part in the peace negotiations leading to the treaty of 1630 with Spain, and was appointed Groom of the Bedchamber, which brought ancillary income from sources such as the collection of fines in the Star Chamber. Elected an MP in 1640, he was one of the eleven men whom Parliament was unwilling to pardon after the Civil War. He then lived in exile in the Spanish Netherlands (modern Belgium). Porter was one of Herrick's patrons.

soyled: manured.

compost: preparation.

hind: rustic fellow.

portion: source of wealth.

kine: cattle.

twelve-tide: the Feast of Epiphany, twelve days after Christmas.

fox i' th' hole: a hopping game played by boys.

trammel net: a fine-meshed net for catching fish or birds.

cockrood: a run for snaring woodcocks.

husbandmen: farmers

Cætera desunt: (Latin) 'The rest is wanting'. Suggests that the poem was cut at this point.

What kind of Mistress he would have (p.83)

Lucrece: see p.110

Thais: a famous Greek *hetaera* or courtesan, who lived during the lifetime of Alexander the Great and accompanied him on campaign. She is reputed to have convinced Alexander to burn down the palace of Persepolis, and was the first – after Alexander – to throw a torch into the building. She later became Queen-consort to Ptolemy I, King of Egypt.

A Paranetical, or Advisive Verse... (p.84-5)

Title: *paranetical* – a hortatory text. A paranesis consists of a series of ethical admonitions. The word is derived from the Greek for 'advise', and is mostly used in exegeses of the *New Testament*.

adulce: almost certainly 'sweeten', cf Spanish *dulce* (sweet), *adulçar* (modern Spanish *adulzar*: to sweeten; to soften).

To Anthea (p.85)

push-pin: a children's game.

bents: bent grasses.

Stool-ball (p.86)

stool-ball: a ball-game, which may be a forerunner of cricket, rounders and baseball. In the original form of the game, the receiver had use his hand to defend his stool – typically hung from a tree, and suspended at about shoulder-height – from a thrown ball, and would score a point for each delivery

until the stool was hit. Bats (shaped like frying-pans) were
introduced at a later date.

tansy: a hardy perennial flowering plant, once used as a flavouring
in puddings and cakes, or as an infusion. Also, a cake made of
eggs, cream, wine, sugar and herbs, including tansy juice.

Proof to no purpose (page 88)
luster: from Latin, *lustrum*, a period of five years .

To Sir John Berkeley, Governor of Exeter (p.89)
Title: Youngest son of Sir Maurice Berkeley, of Bruton, Somerset;
knighted in Berwick in 1638; commander-in-chief of the
Royalist forces in Devon, 1643; he captured Exeter on 4
September 1643 and held it until 13 April, 1646. Created
Baron Berkeley of Stratton, in Cornwall, 1658; died 1678.

progermination: budding out.
circumflanked: surrounded.
itchless: i.e. with no itch for bribes.

The Invitation (p.90)
Lautitious: sumptuous.

Heliogabalus (or Elagabalus): born Varius Avitus Bassus;
Emperor of Rome 215-222 AD. A controversial Emperor, an
enthusiastic sun-worshipper with a confused sexual identity.
He and his mother were murdered, and their bodies thrown
into the Tiber.

Sylla: Lucius Cornelius Sylla, or Sulla (d. 78 BC), Consul of
Rome, General and Dictator; subject of one of Plutarch's
Lives. A ruthless leader when in power (and he was *elected*
to the Dictatorship), his exercise of quasi-imperial power
makes him a forerunner of the Caesars.

maiden's-blush: pink rose.
lar: from Latin *lares*, household gods.
jessamine: a.k.a. false jasmine (*Gelsemium sempervirens*).
larded jet: blacked.
soused: pickled.
neat: cow
beer small as comfort: 'small beer' was beer low in alcohol and, as
such, often served to children and servants.

To Mr Henry Lawes... (p.91)

Title: Henry Lawes (1596-1662) was the brother of William Lawes (q.v. p.117), and the most prolific song-composer in England as well as the composer of masques, such as Milton's *Comus* (1634). He set a number of Herrick's poems.

Lanier: Nicholas Lanier (1588-1666), composer and lutenist, and the first Master of the King's Musick. He wrote the music for two of Ben Jonson's stage works.

Gotier: most likely Jacques Gautier (a.k.a. Gautier d'Angleterre, 1617-1660?) – a French lutenist active in England, but possibly Ennemond Gautier, a.k.a. Gautier de Lyon, who visited England in 1630 and played before King Charles I. Herrick actually spells the name Gotire, but, elsewhere in *Hesperides*, in the poem 'A Lyric to Mirth', he spells it Coteire and adds an erratum note at the beginning of the book altering it to Gotier. From the context it can be assumed that he refers to the same lutenist here, and thus the erratum spelling has been preferred.

Wilson: John Wilson (1595-1674), composer, lutenist and singer. Composer for the King's Men troupe from 1614-1623; member of the King's Musicke, 1635; Gentleman of the Chapel Royal, 1662.

Julia's Churching, or Purification (p.92)

fillitings: the pieces of cloth making up a woman's veil, worn when attending church.

decurted: curtailed, cut short.

Hymen: goddess of marriage and the bridal bed.

epithalamy: epithalamium, wedding song or poem.

Upon M. William Lawes, the rare Musician (p.92)

Title: William Lawes (1602-1645), brother of Henry Lawes (q.v. p.116). Song-writer to the King's Men troupe from 1636, perhaps earlier. Musician-in-ordinary to the King from 1635. He wrote instrumental, vocal and church music as well as works for the stage, and set several of Herrick's poems. He was shot and killed at Chester in 1645 while riding with the King, whose troops were trying to relieve the garrison there. His portrait as a cavalier hangs in the Faculty of Music at Oxford.

Amphion: legendary founder of Thebes, son of Antiope from her
   rape by Zeus. He married Niobe, the daugter of Tantalus,
   the King of Lydia. It was thus that he learned to play his lyre
   in the Lydian mode, and added three extra strings to it.
Terpander: Greek poet and citharode (player of the cithara, or
   lyre) of the early 7th century BC; the legendary founder of
   Greek music.
Orpheus: chief representative of the arts of song and the lyre,
   and a mythical figure whose origins lay in Thrace. He was
   a mystical musician and a priest of Dionysus. From ca. 6th
   century BC he is regarded as one of the great original poets,
   and the inventor of the lyre.

A Thanksgiving to God for his House (p.96-97)
spars: roof-beams
buttery: pantry
unflea'd: free of vermin
pulse: bean
worts: herbs
purslain: a garden herb; an annual plant (*Portulaca oleracea*),
   sometimes used as a pot herb and for salads, garnishes, and
   pickles.
kine: cattle

To his Sweet Saviour (p.98)
axletree: A crossbar or rod under a cart, which has spindles at the
   ends, on which the wheels turn.

Mr Robert Herrick his farewell unto Poetry (p.99-101)
bell-man: nightwatchman
firedrake: mythological creature – the Teutonic equivalent of the
   dragon.
ceareclothes: waterproof, waxed cloth used for burial shrouds.
Musaeus: mythical first poet of ancient Greece, pupil or son of
   Orpheus.
Maro: Virgil, whose full name was Publius Vergilius Maro.
minstrel: i.e. Orpheus.
Eurydice: in Greek mythology, a nymph who was the wife of
   Orpheus. While running away from Aristaeus, she was bitten
   by a snake and died. Stricken by his loss, Orpheus went to the

underworld in search of his wife and sang so piteously that even the Furies wept. He was permitted to take her back to the land of the living, provided that he walked in front of her and did not look back. When he disobeyed this instruction, Eurydice vanished.

Grecian orator: i.e. Cicero (106–43BC), considered the greatest orator of ancient Rome, and one of the foremost Latin prose writers.

Attica: Greece.

Tully: Cicero, whose full name was Marcus Tullius Cicero.

Helicon: Mount Helicon in Boeotia, famous in Greek mythology as the location of two springs sacred to the Muses, and mentioned by Hesiod – the earliest of the Greek poets whose work is still extant. Helicon thus became a symbol of poetic inspiration.

Epitaph on the Tomb of Sir Edward Giles... (p.102)
The only epitaph in Herrick's church of St George the Martyr known to have been composed by the poet.

Selected bibliography:
Robert Herrick: *Hesperides: or, The Works Both Humane and Divine of Robert Herrick Esq.* (London, 1648. Facsimile edition of the same: The Scolar Press, Menston, 1969).

The Poems of Robert Herrick (Oxford University Press, World's Classics Series, London, 1902, reset 1933).

Anthologies:
Peter Davidson (ed.): *Poetry and Revolution* (Oxford University Press, Oxford, 1998).

Hugh Maclean (ed.): *Ben Jonson and the Cavalier Poets* (Norton, New York & London, 1974).

H.R. Woudhuysen (ed.): *Penguin Book of Renaissance Verse 1509-1659* (Penguin Books, London & New York, 1992).

Critical:
Roger B. Rollin: *Robert Herrick* (Twayne Publishers, New York, 2nd, revised edition, 1992).

Lightning Source UK Ltd.
Milton Keynes UK
UKOW050854140112

185369UK00001B/6/A